gretchen kingsley

D0696032

Deaf Diaspora

Deaf Diaspora

The Third Wave of Deaf Ministry

Bob Ayres
DeafYouth Ministries/DTQuest

With personal narratives by Chad Entinger

iUniverse, Inc.
New York Lincoln Shanghai

Deaf Diaspora
The Third Wave of Deaf Ministry

All Rights Reserved © 2004 by Robert E. Ayres

No part of this book may be reproduced or transmitted in any form or by any means, graphic, electronic, or mechanical, including photocopying, recording, taping, or by any information storage retrieval system, without the written permission of the publisher.

iUniverse, Inc.

For information address:
iUniverse, Inc.
2021 Pine Lake Road, Suite 100
Lincoln, NE 68512
www.iuniverse.com

ISBN: 0-595-33541-1

Printed in the United States of America

Deaf Diaspora: The Third Wave of Deaf Ministry is a book about ministry to a scattered people in a new millennium. It addresses the question, "How do we reach a new generation of Deaf teenagers with the gospel of Jesus Christ?" The author, Bob Ayres, is co-founder and president of DeafYouth Ministries. Throughout the book are personal narratives by one of the leading Deaf ministers to teenagers in the country, Chad Entinger. Each chapter concludes with a discussion guide for students or small groups.

In the first section, Deaf DIASPORA, the author explores the historical dynamics and impact of Diaspora on a cultural group; illustrates the spiritual legacy in Deaf-World; describes the speed and intensity of the changes in Deaf-World since the 1980s; identifies the resulting spiritual crisis in the Deaf community and presents a definition for a New Culture of Deafness.

In the second section, Waves THREE, ten defining traits are described from two eras of Deaf ministry during the final decades of the 20th Century. Examples are given of First Wave (1960s and 1970s) and Second Wave (1980s and 1990s) ministries. The vital traits of Third Wave (2000s and 2010s) are identified and recommendations are made for effective and sustainable Deaf ministry.

In the third section, Vision IMPACT, general youth ministry insights are provided and specific recommendations are made for ministry with Deaf and hard of hearing teenagers. DeafYouth Ministries was established in 2000 to bring together the best of youth and Deaf ministry. DTQuest is an outreach ministry sponsored by DeafYouth Ministries and uniquely built on Third Wave principles. DTQuest is described in-depth including the basics on establishing a local ministry that is both effective and sustainable.

Endorsements

"*Deaf Diaspora* is a unique combination of Deaf history and contemporary Christian ministry. The book provides an analysis of the past as well as a model for the future. The author offers provocative insights on how to interpret the changing Deaf World, especially for those who desire to understand and minister to that World. This work is thoughtful, relevant, and engaging for those involved in Christian ministry to members of the Deaf Community."
Kent R. Olney, Ph.D., Professor of Sociology, Olivet Nazarene University, Bourbonnais, Illinois

"I was born during the 1970s and became a child of the 1980s. I remember going to the Sunday school classes at my church without a sign language interpreter. I had no clue what my class instructor was saying. I followed wherever the kids went. I had to read the instructor's lips while the other kids closed their eyes and bowed down their heads. Eventually, in the late 80s and early 90s, I finally met a Deaf pastor at my church. He had experience in Deaf ministry. When he started to teach in American Sign Language about the Bible, it opened my spirit, soul and mind. It helped me understand and build a relationship with God. I will never forget that day. Now, it is my turn to take the responsibilities to do the ministry of the Third Wave and *Deaf Diaspora* will be a great guidebook as I become a sensitive Deaf leader for the Deaf teenage population."
Craig Lemak, Area Coordinator, DTQuest-Greater Louisville, Kentucky

"Deaf Ministry is alive! Like all living things, it changes, and Bob Ayres clearly shows the changes in Deaf Ministry over the past forty years and, more importantly, the changes that are happening now and will be happening in the future. *Deaf Diaspora* is a "must read" for anyone who is active in or serving a Deaf Christian ministry, whether it is a stand-alone Deaf church, an interpreted ministry, a small group of Deaf believers or anyone else who has a heart for Jesus and the Deaf."
Mark Seeger, Pastor, Jesus Lutheran Church of the Deaf, Austin, Texas
Pastoral Advisor, International Lutheran Deaf Association

"In this book Brother Ayres shows an unusually keen knowledge of the past, a strong sensitivity with the present and a proposed plan for the future…all in order to best reach deaf people for Jesus. The book is proving to be an invaluable aid as we train students to minister among deaf people. Ayres excels at evaluating the current situation of deaf people in America, and analyzing how the situation came about and where it may lead."
Duane King, Executive Director, Deaf Missions, Council Bluffs, Iowa

"Bob Ayres has put together a book that is deeply challenging to anyone in Deaf Ministry. The days when deaf churches exists side-by-side with deaf schools are over. Instead of dreaming for "the good old days" to return, Bob invites us to move on and contextualize the Gospel to make it clear to Deaf people in *today's* circumstances. He's right on."
Chip Green, Founder, The Tenth Coin, Batavia, New York

"Periodically, something comes across my desk that has major significance in terms of raising my own personal consciousness regarding the needs and experiences of deaf culture. In the last ten years, only two scholarly, excellent presentations have been printed that caught my attention. One of the two is this book. Through this manuscript, I have been made more aware of the significant changes within deaf culture, and have been challenged in my own personal response to those changes. For someone who desires to understand these issues, *Deaf Diaspora* will do more than raise a few eyebrows; it will invite introspection and personal reflection. My thanks go to Bob Ayres and Chad Entinger for their invaluable contribution to the field of deaf ministry with this book. Like the old shaving lotion commercial of an earlier day, a fresh splash of cold water hitting our faces only encourages us to say, "Thanks, Bob! We needed that!"
Rick McClain, Deaf Pastor, College Church of the Nazarene, Olathe, Kansas

"In the 1980s I served as a chaplain at a residential school for the deaf and was able to provide religious activities both on and off campus. At that time, it was easy to plan retreats, camps and other activities on the weekends and have large groups in attendance. However, my colleagues and I noticed a growing trend to educationally mainstream deaf children and many of us became concerned. What was to become of these mainstreamed deaf children spiritually? How were they to learn about Jesus? How were they to develop a deaf identity? I moved on to teach in a Bible College program for the Deaf and these concerns remained a burden on my heart. The situation seemed hopeless. I despaired that God would hold us accountable for a lost generation of deaf people. Bob Ayres' book gives me hope for the first time. He addresses these issues clearly and forthrightly. Bob offers a

plan of action that is already proving effective across the country. God has clearly inspired Bob to write this book for precisely 'such a time as this.'"
Mary J. High, Ph.D., Associate Professor of American Sign Language, Gardner-Webb University, Boiling Springs, North Carolina

"This is a very exciting book, because it centers Deaf culture just where it should be: in Jesus. This book discusses the history, present, and future of Deaf Culture from a Christian perspective and it is long overdue. Not only that, it is an instruction manual on how to reach out to today's Deaf teenagers with the Gospel of Jesus Christ. And that's a real gift to us, who have the heart and drive to do His work in today's changing times. How do we maintain our identity and culture in the midst of such change and remain faithful to Christ Jesus? I was one of those Deaf teenagers that grew up mainstreamed, who was blessed enough to have a family who was willing to do anything it took for me to learn about Jesus. This included learning signs, becoming immersed in Deaf culture, and doing anything it took for me to know Jesus as my personal Savior. Not only that, my faith was certainly *caught* from all the different role models I had growing up. God sure was looking out for me. (Jeremiah 29:11) But there was a problem. I didn't have Deaf Christian peers. I had Deaf friends, but no Deaf Christian ones, and that was hard. I didn't know where to look, and I didn't know where to find them. It took a long time, and I think that as much as my family gave me, I needed Deaf Christian peers to truly understand my identity as a Deaf individual, as who God created me to be. That's why working with DTQuest is such a privilege, because I am seeing God work in the hearts of these Deaf teens. I am seeing hearts born again, becoming living miracles for Christ. I am seeing not just one, not just two but many Deaf teens gathering together and enjoying fellowship together. Not only are they learning about God, they are learning *together—growing together as the body of Christ!* Don't tell me that Deaf Culture isn't alive and well, because it sure is, and Jesus is glorified by it."
Matthew Reynolds, Area Coordinator, DTQuest Greater Portland/Vancouver, Beaverton, Oregon

"As I read through the pages of *Deaf Diaspora*, my heart is stirred and excited at the vision that is cast before my eyes for the future of Deaf ministry. Bob Ayres does a wonderful job describing the past, present and future of a unique and diverse culture while connecting it to a relevant relational Christ-centered ministry to Deaf teens. Chad Entinger's personal narratives give a true inside look at the changing dynamics of Deaf culture and ministry. As Chad shares his life experiences along side the depth of knowledge in each chapter leads the reader to a greater understanding of the need to examine their own ministry to the Deaf.

Working with Deaf teens on a daily basis, it is exciting for me to see a framework and guide to take Jesus to the hearts of the next generation of Deaf leaders. Many thanks go to Bob for his willingness and courageous spirit to follow God's leading in writing this book."
Chris McGaha, Chaplain, Alabama Institute for the Deaf and Blind, Talladega, Alabama.

"Three Cheers for Bob Ayres! I got a rare opportunity to sit down and listen to his lecture on his upcoming book *Deaf Diaspora* and can attest to his astounding breadth of knowledge! This book is a fresh view and insight on what has happened in reaching out towards the deaf community for Christ and the struggles that have come with it. Bob comes up with a proposal that is able to keep up with the changing times in order to have a future in bringing our deaf youth to Christ! Bob is a very humble man whose heart is great in heeding God's call to reach out towards the deaf youth, after all, we as Christians are only a generation away from extinction. Here is a man who has set up DeafTeen Quest across the nation, bringing people together for the glory of our Lord. He seeks nothing but to exalt the name of Jesus through teaching others on reaching out towards the deaf youth. This is a wonderful example from Ephesians 4:4, *'There is one body, and one Spirit, even as ye are called in one hope of your calling'* where both the deaf and the hearing are working together for the love for our Lord! Again, I say, Three Cheers for Bob Ayres!"
Dirk R. Albrecht, Area Coordinator, DTQ-Central Maryland, Frederick, Maryland and Dean of Students, Maryland School for the Deaf

Abbreviations for Bible translations

NIV	New International Version of the Bible
NASB	New American Standard Bible
NLT	New Living Translation
CEV	Contemporary English Version
NKJV	New King James Version

Contents

Preface

This is first and foremost, a book about ministry to a scattered people. The focus is on reaching a new generation of Deaf and hard of hearing individuals with the gospel of Jesus Christ. This generation can loosely be defined as those born after the advent of Public Law 94-142 in 1975. They were in their middle 20s or younger at the turn of the century. For most in this age category, their experience of deafness is dramatically different from those who are older. However, many of the principles of relational ministry found here apply to Deaf ministry with individuals of any age.

Effective ministry recognizes the culture of the people it serves. The Deaf community of the new century is radically different from even twenty years ago. At the outset of building sustainable ministry, it is important to recognize these incredible changes and the need to adapt. The Deaf community now, more than ever, faces this difficult challenge for cultural survival. Those involved in Deaf ministry must think in new ways for bringing together the scattered Deaf community with this life-changing, eternal gospel of our Lord.

There are two key words relevant to understanding Diaspora: **enculturation** and **acculturation**. *Enculturation* is the process by which one becomes part of his or her own native culture. It involves intentional efforts to keep a culture alive throughout time. *Acculturation* is the process of adopting the cultural patterns of another group. It is "a process of social change caused by the interaction of significantly diverse cultures."[1] Enculturation encourages being *set apart* while acculturation results in *blending in*. The survival of a minority cultural group, such as the Deaf community, depends on the balance of these two variables.

One of the primary issues facing Deaf people in contemporary society is the challenge of maintaining a viable "Deaf-World."[2] The combined words Deaf-World are the English language equivalency for the American Sign Language (ASL) signs describing the entire experience of being Deaf and part of the Deaf community. This is the term I use to describe the cultural group commonly referred to as the Deaf community. The concept originates within Deaf community for describing their unique world.

Nearly everything has changed in the Deaf-World *except the reality of the need all people have for a personal and meaningful relationship with God*. This one thing remains constant. We will explore a new paradigm in Deaf ministry for the new millennium. For effective and sustainable impact in the lives of Deaf individuals, those involved in Deaf ministry need to…

- recapture the rich faith traditions of Deaf-World through team based relational ministry that responds to the spiritual needs of the next generation
- create new opportunities for Deaf to gather, interact, and connect with each other for enculturation of Deaf culture to continue and flourish
- adapt to the inevitable acculturation of language and culture with the dominant hearing world due to the scattering of the Deaf community
- recognize the authenticity of a New Culture of Deafness that is emerging in the 21st Century in the United States

There are a number of new concepts presented in this book and a redefinition of some old concepts. There are sections in this book that may create controversy because of a departure from previously held beliefs in certain academic circles. For too long, a small group of people have framed up the discussion about the characteristics of Deaf-World that excludes huge numbers of people who legitimately belong within this community. This book presents a fresh and inclusive perspective on the emerging new Deaf culture for the purpose of effectively ministering with and to this next generation.

Although it is a departure from conventional rules of grammar with regards to capitalization, I have chosen to capitalize the letter "D" in deaf when referring to any individual who has a hearing loss that has a significant impact on the tasks of daily living. The reason is to identify deafness as a cultural experience such as being African-American, Native American, or Jewish. It allows one to designate the group (signified by the capital letter) and the individual as part of the group. I use the designation "hard of hearing" (lower case without hyphens) to designate individuals who have some level of functional hearing but are still affected by their deafness. I use the lower case with the word "deafness" and in places where the sentence is referring to a physical characteristic (i.e. "He was born deaf.") and not specifically cultural connections. I ask forgiveness of those who disagree with these decisions based on either grammatical rules or a fundamental disagreement with my logic about the nature of culture. When quoting a source, I use the terminology as found.

Any Deaf or hard of hearing person in this book is referred to as "Deaf" regardless of his or her preferred mode of communication, level of hearing loss or cultural background. In stark contrast to the exclusivity of many in the secular world, the Christian faith is more inclusive and welcoming with regards to Deaf-

World. All are created equal in the image of God. A person is welcomed as a member of the Deaf community (with a capital "D") if she or he primarily gathers information through sight instead of sound.

I also struggled with the issue of writing in the proper tense. My goal for this manuscript is to serve as a textbook on Deaf ministry in the 21st Century, so whenever possible I wrote in an objective, third person tense. At the same time, this book is intended to be readable and full of personal stories, insights, and illustrations from ministry experiences that are best read in the more friendly first person style. My conclusion was to write with a mix of both. Again, I ask for understanding from those whom this might bother. As a general rule, I try to communicate information about historical patterns and events in third person and move into first person when expressing how this information is applied in ministry. In effect, the first person tense notes that my role has shifted from an observer of historical patterns to an instructor of those involved in Deaf ministry.

Regarding my use of the term *Christian*, there is not general agreement about who this includes and excludes in popular usage. I rarely use this term in the broadest sense to refer to the historic religion that includes every faith movement that traces its roots to Jesus of Nazareth. There are also a number of denominations and loosely associated churches that use the word *Christian* in their name to describe themselves. I use the term *Christian* to refer to any who have a personal experience of faith in Jesus Christ as Lord and Savior. This is commonly referred to as people who have had a personal *conversion* experience.[3] This person may be and remain a member of any one of hundreds of distinct denominations (including Roman Catholic, Orthodox, Protestant, and others) but the common characteristic is the recognition of an individual need for a personal relationship with God that is only possible through the sacrifice of Jesus Christ, a desire to build one's faith on the Bible and a passion to mature in this relationship through God's grace. Some refer to these followers of Christ as *born-again*,[4] others call this group of people the *remnant*[5] and many like the terms *evangelicals*[6] or *believers*.[7] Personally, I may use any one of these terms but most of the time will use the general term *Christian* to refer to those who know Christ as personal Savior and Lord. I am reminded of the Scripture where Jesus said, *"I am the good shepherd; I know my sheep and my sheep know me, just as the Father knows me and I know the Father and I lay down my life for the sheep. I have other sheep that are not of this sheep pen. I must bring them also. They too will listen to my voice, and there shall be one flock and one shepherd."* (John 10:14-16, NIV)

Appreciation is expressed to my colleague and friend, Chad Entinger, for his role in the formation of this book and willingness to contribute personal narratives that provide valuable insight. My lifelong friend, Ben Sharpton—a much better writer than I—has been a great source of encouragement (and challenge).

My deepest appreciation to Tim Bender, Colin Bruner, David Cannon, Chip Green, Dr. Mary High, Cathy Howle, Duane King, Rick McClain, Dr. Kent Olney, Matthew Reynolds, and Robert Schniedewind for important feedback and review of the manuscript before publication. Thanks to all my Deaf friends who continue to teach me so much but especially to the Penland family for loving us and introducing us to the Deaf-World back in the early 1980s. To all the DTQuest leaders and committee members and most importantly, the Deaf teenagers…you are the reason this book has been such an important priority of mine. I hope you are ultimately the beneficiaries of this labor.

DeafYouth Ministries would not exist without an awesome Board of Trustees. I will only mention Sue Rueff, Deedee Rietze, Linda Rueff and Marvin Highfill (although each member is vital) because of the significant role each has played in this national ministry. My children, Christina, David, Casey, John and Ana have all been patient with my time at the computer on this project. My daughter Ana (who is Deaf) is a great instructor of her parents and siblings as well. Finally, my wife and best friend for over a quarter of a century, Kathy Casey Ayres, has incredible editing skills, a loving heart and keen intellect; she is my soul mate. To God is all glory for everything we share.

Come on! Let's journey together as we find our path into the future. Join in as we build a sense of oneness again. May God bless your reading of this book and may we help you effectively minister to the next generation of Deaf young people!

Bob Ayres
DeafYouth Ministries
www.dtquest.org
www.bobayres.com

Deaf DIASPORA
Section I

Chapter 1—Scattered Community

Diaspora refers to a scattering or dispersion of a culture group.

Di·as·po·ra (*noun*)

1. A general term to indicate the widespread settlement of Jews outside of Palestine. The most significant scattering of this people group were from the conquering of the Jews by the Assyrian and Babylonian empires.[8]

2. Scattering of any group, particularly those with a language and cultural identity; a dispersion of an originally homogeneous group: "the Diaspora of the Deaf community was largely the result of educational mainstreaming."[9]

The term "Diaspora" may be unfamiliar to you. Those with a background in theology or history will likely recognize the word. The meaning is rooted in a specific historic event that is still evident today: the scattering of the Jewish people around the world. However, it applies to any people group with a similar language and culture who are dispersed or scattered.

The Deaf community has always been scattered across the United States but brought together as an identifiable cultural group by the residential schools for the Deaf or, if they are students in a mainstreamed school program, by the use of American Sign Language as their chosen mode of communication. Until the middle 1970s, a high percentage of these individuals would travel to the schools for the Deaf and would come home only a few times each year. Historically, the Deaf community was perpetuated primarily through connection with the schools of the Deaf. They were the source of Deaf culture, language, arts, and the general connection with the larger Deaf community. Students often developed a strong sense of identity and connection within these residential schools and regarded other students, faculty and staff as a surrogate family. The school represented a type of "homeland" where Deaf language, culture, experiences, stories, humor and history were perpetuated from one generation to the next. Through various relationships developed at the schools, religious beliefs and traditions were also passed down along with the fullness of Deaf culture.

Deaf people are generally scattered from birth due to the random nature of deafness. By far, most deaf individuals are born into hearing families where deafness is not an inherited trait.[10] Deafness is most often the result of a medical incident such as a high fever, encephalitis, rubella measles, or a severe ear infection. Usually, the individual is the "only Deaf" in a hearing family and will likely have hearing offspring. Surprisingly, the vast majority has hearing parents (and will have hearing children) and fewer than ten percent of these parents are fluent in sign language.[11] This means that for their deaf children to find connections with the Deaf community, these hearing parents must venture into somewhat uncomfortable territory where they often feel awkward and intimidated. As a result, there is not a natural connection for many children born deaf and many barriers must be overcome to gather as a community.

With the advent of mainstreaming and later the Americans with Disabilities Act (ADA), this dispersed community remained scattered in their local areas and school systems rather than gathered at residential schools. The rights contained in the ADA also created more opportunities for employment in locations other than traditional work sites for Deaf employees. Some residential schools for the Deaf have been closed down and most have dramatically decreased in the number of students. This has created a tremendous scattering of deaf and hard of hearing students who have lost not only a sense of connection but also identification with cultural deafness. The Deaf community is now facing an unprecedented crisis largely as a result of this dispersion. Diaspora usually implies a scattering against the will of the community such as is experienced by a conquered people. This dispersion is the result of decisions made by the dominant hearing community. The reality is this Deaf Diaspora has brought about a crisis of culture, language, relationships and faith.

Briefly considered are four examples of other communities who experienced Diaspora. The lessons learned from their experiences can be applied to Deaf ministry in the 21st Century as we struggle to find balance between effective enculturation[1] and successful acculturation[2]. What are the general choices that either strengthened or weakened these communities? How does a people group maintain a unique cultural identity while being assimilated into the mainstream of a majority population? How does a cultural group pass on traditions, language, his-

---

[1] Enculturation is the process by which one becomes part of his or her own native culture.

[2] Acculturation is the process of adopting the cultural patterns of another group.

tory, values, and priorities to new generations of young people who are being raised as part of another dominant culture? How can people of one culture take advantage of opportunities provided by another culture without losing original cultural connections and identity?

Historic Examples of Diaspora

The Northern and Southern Kingdoms of Israel, the Native Americans on our continent and the African-Americans are specific examples of unique ethnic groups who each faced the challenge of Diaspora. Each group struggled to maintain their identity, language and culture while living as a scattered people. Some were more successful than others. Note the impact of the balance or imbalance of enculturation and acculturation in each of the groups. There are literally thousands of cultures over the years who have experienced Diaspora but these are four examples that illustrate this point. Each holds a lesson for the Deaf community.

Northern Kingdom of Israel—Following the rule of King Solomon, the Jewish nation entered a time of civil war and ultimately was divided into two countries; Israel in the north and Judah in the south. In 721 B.C., Assyria conquered the ten tribes of the north and completely dispersed this Jewish population across the region. They never recovered from this Diaspora and essentially ceased to exist as part of Jewish history. It is from the intermarriage of these Jews with other foreign people groups that the Samaritans of the New Testament emerged. They also adopted many of the false idols and beliefs of the foreign cultures. By the time of Christ, the more traditional and conservative Jews in the south looked down upon this group as a mixed-race, apostate people who abandoned their heritage. The Northern Tribes of Israel are an example of a people group that moved into cultural extinction by *total acculturation*; blending into the dominant culture without maintaining a unique identity.

Southern Kingdom of Judah—The current-day Jews and the Israeli nation are the spiritual, social, physical and cultural descendents of the Southern Kingdom of Judah. These are the Jews we read about in the New Testament accounts during the time of Jesus. The two southern tribes who primarily made up the Southern Kingdom were taken into exile by the Babylonians in 598 and 587 B.C. and then allowed to return to Palestine after about seventy years of captivity. Although they were taken into exile, this group was able to maintain their unique identity as Jews. They kept their traditions even during this time of oppression and slavery. They continued to marry and bear children within their own community. When they returned to Palestine, they were able to reestablish their system of government. They rebuilt the temple. Even after the Romans conquered Jerusalem in 63 B.C. they were able to define themselves clearly as Jews who were the "people of the covenant."[12]

There was an uprising by the Jews in 66 A.D. against the Roman occupation of their country. This led to the total destruction of Jerusalem in 70 A.D., including the center of Jewish life, Solomon's Temple. From that point on, the Jews were unable to reestablish a homeland until the middle of the 20th Century. They were scattered throughout the world. From the destruction of the Temple until the establishment of Israel in 1948, the Jewish people had to live in small communities across the world. Amazingly, the descendents of these Jews were able to maintain a distinct identity as a unique cultural, language and religious group even after all these years. They survived a brutal Holocaust during World War II where over six million Jews were executed. They have been amazingly effective in maintaining their cultural and religious identity throughout history with a mixture of *enculturation* and *acculturation* to other societies.

Native Americans—Native Americans are another group to face the challenge of maintaining a unique identity within their own communities. In 1492, when Christopher Columbus first arrived in the Americas there were an estimated five million Native Americans on this northern continent who were descendents of people who had inhabited these lands for at least ten thousand years. By 1900, this Native American population had decreased to 237,000.[13] At one time in California, ordered by the Governor, there was a bounty paid for the scalps or ears of Indians. In 1814, the Creek Nation lost twenty-two million acres to the dominant U.S. forces in Georgia and parts of Alabama. The most infamous act was the "Indian Removal Act of 1830" by then President Andrew Jackson to move the entire Cherokee Nation from the southeastern states (primarily Georgia where the Cherokee Nation capital was located in New Echota) to present-day Oklahoma. 4,000 men, women, and children died on this thousand-mile march of a total of 15,000 people. This is painfully remembered as the "Trail of Tears."[14] In mainstream society, there is little left intact other than Indian names and landmarks.[15]

The Native American Diaspora was different from the African-American experience because they were kept more intact but isolated on lands that are legally separate nations within our borders called "reservations." Those who survived the genocide of the earlier centuries in our country found themselves isolated and marginalized from the mainstream society-at-large. The consequences of this isolation are dramatic. Unemployment in these Native American communities is staggering and requires large outlays of public funding in response.[16] Alcoholism and self-destructive behavior is a tremendous problem in many of these communities. Estimates are that three of four Native American homes are directly affected by alcoholism. The suicide rate is the highest of any ethnic group in our country.[17] Many tribes cling to the traditions and languages of their people in these very small pockets but face the ongoing challenge of eventual total extinction of their tribal identity. Those who leave the reservations and are acculturated into the larger society find it difficult to live in two disparate worlds.

Native Americans lived on the American continents for thousands of years before first contact with Europeans. Some of these tribes became powerful and well-organized with extensive governmental and community structures. Over the past 500 years, primarily due to wars with the European expansionists, genocide, and policies that displaced and oppressed the native peoples, American Indians have been either culturally obliterated or isolated. There are still 562 identifiable Native American tribes in existence today "recognized and eligible for funding and services from the Bureau of Indian Affairs by virtue of their status as Indian tribes."[18] Many of these tribes live on reservations with their own language, culture, and economy. There are approximately fifty-six million acres of Indian land within the borders of the United States.[19] In the 2000 Census, over forty of these tribes had at least 7000 respondents each claiming tribal connections.[20] This radical isolation, largely imposed by outside factors, has led to virtual extinction within the larger society; these numbers reflect only 1% of our overall population. Native Americans who remain on the reservations are largely deprived the benefits of the larger society. Many tribes have been able to maintain their language and customs but are facing extinction due to the gap between their isolated world (strict enculturation) and mainstream society. Others with Native American roots have experienced cultural extinction through total acculturation into mainstream American. This is an example of *strict enculturation* and *total acculturation* leading to extinction.[21]

African-Americans—The first Africans arrived in bondage in the Virginia Colony in 1619. The oppression and cruelty of slavery is well-known in our American society so will not be chronicled here. The African-American community faced a Diaspora that broke apart tribes, communities, and even families. The unique cruelty of this type of slavery created an incredible challenge for the African community to overcome. In many ways, they serve as the best model for the Deaf community to emulate.

Within the African-American community, tremendous effort has been given to maintaining a definitive cultural identity. There are African-American neighborhoods, colleges, scholarships, clubs, churches, music companies, advertising agencies, etc. As a community, African-Americans constantly work to overcome oppression and communicate the values of the community. One example of effective efforts at African-American enculturation is Kwanzaa, a cultural festival, conceived and developed by Dr. Maulana Ron Karenga in 1966. Kwanzaa seeks to promote a connection with African cultural identity for people scattered around the world.[22] The goal of Kwanzaa is to instill a pride in African heritage that strengthens one's connection with the larger culture.

Though most African-Americans are unfamiliar with the original languages of their native continent, there has been a new cultural language developed here in the United States. It is often referred to as "Black English" or Ebonics. Ebonics does not find full acceptance within the mainstream educational system but is certainly a part of the African-American experience. African-Americans become essentially bilingual and bicultural. They are able to maintain cultural identity while adapting to the language and culture of the overall society. This common language helps connect a scattered people. At the same time, the African-American community has been effective in assimilation into the mainstream American experience through education, military service, sports, entertainment, and the overall impact of the Civil Rights movement. They have effectively blended together *enculturation* and *acculturation*. This approach has led to a sense of pride and inclusion even though discrimination persists in our society.

What do we observe about the experiences of these four dispersed cultures?

Northern Tribes of Israel—lost language, culture and religious identity; never regained homeland; ceased to exist as a definable people group.
This is an example of total acculturation <u>without</u> enculturation.
The Result?—Total cultural extinction

Southern Tribes of Judah—lost language (later reclaimed Hebrew as the official language in Israel); maintained culture and religious identity in various countries; finally regained homeland after almost 1900 years.
This is an example of enculturation <u>with</u> limited acculturation.
The Result?—Survival and reestablishment of nation of Israel; they also were able to exist as a strong (and diverse) religious and cultural group in various nations over the past 2000 years of Diaspora.

Native Americans—maintained culture, language, and religious identity in isolation; never truly regained homeland although they were assigned designated areas as sovereign lands.
This is an example of strict enculturation <u>and</u> total acculturation.
The Result?—Widespread extinction through the extremes of isolation on sovereign lands or, in contrast, the total loss of cultural identity as part of mainstream culture.

African-Americans—lost native language but mastered new language, created a new variation on traditional English language, allowed culture to evolve;

developed cohesive religious identities; never regained homeland but became full citizens of a new land.

This is an example of effective enculturation __with__ effective acculturation

The Result?—Establishment of new culture in a new environment although barriers continue to be faced.

Drawing from these examples, one may observe that the successful continuation of a culture is most likely by avoiding the extremes of *strict enculturation* (isolation) and *total acculturation* (extinction); adapting to allow for survival as a cultural group without a loss of a collective identity. Likewise, the cultural identity may evolve but will need to remain identifiable in some way. Those cultures who survive seem to share a common trait of being intentional in efforts to keep the culture alive. Cultures do not continue through neglect; those who are within the culture must find ways to pass along this culture to the next generations.

Living in the Hearing World

Extensive research has been completed on the sociological aspects of deafness as a definable cultural experience.[23] There are some very strong positions presented in numerous books as to the distinctiveness of the Deaf culture. The discussion usually revolves around the language, values, and traditions of the Deaf community. A few of the foundational questions presented by this book are: What is the key characteristic of a community that binds together all other traits? What is the cornerstone characteristic of a definable cultural group? What sociological aspect of deafness provides the "glue" for holding together the Deaf community for the future?

Strict enculturation leads to the disappearance of a cultural group. Some in the Deaf community seem to despise all things "hearing." They want to interact only within the core Deaf culture. They reject other Deaf people who "think hearing." This type of isolation will not benefit the Deaf community. A cultural minority group must learn to live and thrive in the dominant society. There is no way to return to an earlier era in Deaf-World. The Deaf community must work, study, live, interact, socialize, purchase from, sell to, and communicate with those in the majority hearing population. The Deaf community needs to be aware of the same potential danger of cultural isolation.

Total acculturation leads to the assimilation and ultimate extinction of a cultural group. This is what happened to the Northern Tribes of Israel. If the hearing world is allowed to view deafness as primarily a physical disability, then there is a general disregard of the cultural aspects of being Deaf. Within this paradigm, people with a hearing loss become "hearing impaired" and are defined only in relation to the hearing world. Efforts are made to erase deafness as a disability. The pathological view of deafness seeks the "cure" of hearing loss and the destruction of the Deaf identity.

Both *strict enculturation* and *total acculturation* ultimately lead to the obliteration of an identifiable cultural group within a dominant society. The answer exists between these two extremes. The Deaf community must adapt to the majority population without losing a sense of its unique, historic traits. We must recognize the reality of the new challenges of the 21st Century and develop a new understanding of what it means to be part of the Deaf culture—a member of *Deaf-World*.

Most Deaf children are born into a hearing family. A study by the Gallaudet Research Institute claims that "*less than five percent* of Deaf and hard of hearing students receiving special education are known to have at least one deaf parent…"[24] This vast majority of Deaf children are faced with the challenge of developing an identity as someone who is part of two worlds. They love their families yet feel an inherent and painful separation from them. As children, they often feel like strangers in their own households. Many Deaf children and youth have significant friendships with hearing peers yet often experience frustrating isolation from larger group interactions. Hard of hearing people, in particular, may experience this tug in two directions. It is a huge challenge to maintain a cohesive cultural identity while living as a scattered people. The challenge is developing a positive self-concept while actively interacting with the hearing world. Many young Deaf people express the feeling of being caught between two worlds; hearing and Deaf. This is especially true if they have a cochlear implant or some level of functional hearing that may be assisted with the use of a hearing aid, or some other assistance. There are two basic ways of viewing this situation. Either a person feels part of *neither* culture (negative) or feels connected with *both* cultures (positive).

Binding a Community Together

What is the defining trait that binds a community together? The prevailing wisdom has been maintained that it is a common language, perspectives, or homeland. This certainly makes sense from a sociological perspective. However, it is time to question these assumptions with regards to Deaf ministry. A case needs to be made that historically, none of these have been vital to the survival of a people group.

The first impulse in Deaf ministry is often, "Language! American Sign Language is what defines culturally Deaf people!" According to one source, "It is through their language that Deaf people maintain their identification as a culturally distinct group."[25] The example of the Jewish people and the African-Americans seems to contradict that the defining trait of a cultural group is a common language. The Jews did not (and do not) share a common language universally. Hebrew, the official language of current day Israel, was not in common use for many years, especially during the Middle Ages, and had to be reestablished as a living language. Most Jews in countries other than Israel do not speak Hebrew fluently and only use it during religious services. In the African Diaspora, most African-Americans or those who live in other non-African countries speak no Swahili or any of the diverse African languages. In the United States, Ebonics may be a recognizable language, but it does not *define* the African-American experience. American Sign Language is the native language of the Deaf community but not necessarily of the individual Deaf person. Fluency in American Sign Language is *not* the defining trait of membership in the Deaf-World.

Others may claim, "It is the common perspective. Those who accept the values and beliefs of the community keep the community alive." There are many examples to the contrary. The Jewish people are as diverse a group of people as any in the history of the world. There is a Jewish saying, "When you have three Jews in a room, you get five points of view." It defines the strength, definitiveness and diversity of the Jewish people. Today, there are nineteen different political parties who make up the membership of the Israeli Parliament, the Knesset.[26] Israel is an incredibly diverse country with a united identity. There is great diversity within any ethnic group with regards to opinions, perspectives, beliefs, traditions, preferences, and educational levels. There is no common perspective in the Deaf-World. Although there is a shared experience, there are no actual common values and beliefs. Deaf people are as diverse as any people group in the world. A *common perspective* does not define them as a people.

Is cultural viability based on this common homeland? The schools for the Deaf have been the traditional homeland for the Deaf community. Does the sustainability of Deaf culture depend on the continuation of residential schools of the Deaf? There is evidence in other cultural groups that the homeland can be redefined and exist in a more abstract manner. The Jews survived almost two thousand years without a homeland. Most Jews in the 21st Century do not live in the homeland of Israel. The same is true of the dispersed African community; large numbers of people descendent from the African continent will never live in Africa. Their home is wherever they live. *Homeland* is more of an abstract, emotional connection with a proud legacy and heritage by a people that have overcome persecution and oppression. There is a general sense of connection with others of a similar cultural heritage. Although this has been the case in Deaf-World (literally and figuratively), it is not a homeland that defines the Deaf community, particularly in younger people.

For many, there is no emotional connection with the residential schools yet many are still developing a strong Deaf identity.

For the older generation, a common question asked when meeting a Deaf person for the first time was "Where did you go to school?" meaning, "Which residential school for the Deaf did you attend?" The Deaf Club, a popular gathering of Deaf people in various cities, was largely a by-product of the relationships built at the Deaf schools. This question still holds meaning among older Deaf but with less significance when asked of a younger person. The new generation basically wants to know, "Were you mainstreamed or did you go to the school for the Deaf?" Everyone knows these are two radically different experiences of deafness.

The Deaf-World faces the decision as to how to respond. In today's world and into the future, what truly defines the Deaf community as an identifiable cultural group? Although a few still exist, the days of large, vibrant Deaf schools in every state are gone. The homeland is vanishing, the language is in a state of flux, and whatever shared values existed previously are being greatly altered by more frequent contact with the majority hearing population. This is the stark reality of our society as we enter the 21st century. There is no real prospect of ever turning back the clock. The residential educational setting is a wonderful and vital part of the Deaf legacy. The changes in the educational priorities of our nation are bittersweet for the Deaf community and presents new challenges and opportunities.

There are important aspects of a cultural identity including a common language, similar values, and identifiable homeland. What is the keystone upon which a viable cultural structure is built over the ages? The vital unifying element common in the Jewish, African-American, and Native American experiences, as well as many other cultures that are dispersed, is spiritual faith. Although many want to discount the importance of faith within a community, *the main bond that holds together a cultural group during Diaspora is a foundational belief in a God who will guide them; a God who keeps them united, even while scattered.* Faith in God holds a people together. Spirituality, completely ignored in recent secular literature regarding the Deaf-World, holds the greatest hope for reconnecting the scattered population of Deaf people. There may be tremendous diversity within faith perspectives but cultures that survive Diaspora have a core belief in a Higher Being who offers love, guidance, and definition of them as a people created in God's image and for God's purposes. Religious faith may be the single, greatest definer of values and beliefs even with tremendous diversity among people of a common faith.

The clearest example of the impact of a loss of faith in a cultural group is in the ancient Northern Tribes of Israel. The assimilation of these people and the loss of a Jewish identity are directly related to their loss of observable and transferable faith and historic religious traditions. In the Bible, this is referred to as *apostasy* or chasing after false gods. The stories of their culture continued but the cultural group itself was extinguished. Being a descendent of the "Covenant People"[27] is what defines one as a Jew whether an American, Brazilian, or Norwegian. This was lost by the Northern Tribes and maintained by the Southern Tribes. The Jews active in today's world are all direct descendents of these two Southern Tribes.

There are other examples of the impact of spiritual faith on cultural sustainability. Religion drives societies for better or worse. Every Native American tribe has a spiritual belief at the very center of their existence. The church played a crucial role in helping the African-American community survive through slavery, Jim Crow laws, Civil Rights movement, and in current efforts for full equality and inclusion. The primary civil rights leaders have historically been ministers—including the architect of the movement, a Baptist pastor, Dr. Martin Luther King, Jr. There are examples of a crisis within our society that could be attributed to a loss of religious values. In some cultures, religion has been destructive and violent. Most cultures in the history of the world have a common belief structure about spiritual matters; it is a vital part of what defines a cohesive cultural group. This is especially important during a time of Diaspora.

Spiritual Legacy in the Deaf Community

The Deaf community shares a great spiritual legacy. As in any cultural group, there is diversity of perspectives and beliefs. Every person has an innate sense of wanting to understand ones place in the cosmos. Within the historic Deaf community, there is an identifiable legacy of concern with spiritual things particularly from a Judeo-Christian worldview. The basic perspectives of Judaism and Christianity—the goodness of creation and the sovereignty of God—lends itself naturally to the inclusion of Deaf individuals as full and equal members in the family of God. There is an inherent respectfulness for all creation within the Judeo-Christian worldview. God has created some people Deaf and His creation is perfect. All people, hearing and deaf, are created in the image of God. Each person will sin and fall short of the glory of God but God provides a way to have a personal experience of faith. Faith is experienced in the heart and mind; it exists with equal significance in all languages and cultures. The Deaf community is in no way excluded from this grace.

The Christian perspective, particularly in the evangelical paradigm, believes each person is on equal footing because of a common need for redemption. One cannot be "good enough" to earn salvation. It is a gift. A familiar Christian saying *is the ground is level at the foot of the cross.* Anyone who accepts Christ's atoning death on the cross for personal forgiveness of sin is welcomed equally to God through this sacrifice of Jesus Christ. Galatians 3:28 says there is *"neither Jew nor Greek, slave nor free, male nor female"* when it comes to being equal partners in the kingdom of God, *"for you are all one in Christ Jesus."* For our discussion, we could add *"neither Deaf nor hearing."* As Christians, we participate fully in the body of Christ based on our gifts and talents.

The historic Christian church has put this faith into action. In France, Abbe' Charles Michael de l'Epee (1712-1789), known as the "father of the deaf," (referring to his role as an educator) founded "the first public school for the Deaf in the history of the world."[28] More than two hundred schools were started by either de l'Epee or his disciples. His primary successor, Abbe' Sicard was assisted by his student, Jean Massieu, who was Deaf. Massieu was appointed as the chief teaching assistant for Sicard by Louis XVI.[29] Massieu's student, life-long friend and academic colleague was Laurent Clerc, also Deaf and a significant contributor to Deaf education in the United States. This all came about as a result of commitment to the Deaf by a group of Catholic clerics who "created in turn educated leader(s) among the deaf, instilling in us pride in our language and ourselves, and an elevated vision of what we could become."[30]

In the United States, Reverend Thomas H. Gallaudet was an Episcopal priest who, along with Laurent Clerc and Dr. Mason Cogswell, founded the American School for the Deaf in 1817, as the first permanent public school for the Deaf. What an incredible example of the power of a Deaf educator of the Deaf (Clerc), a parent of a Deaf child (Cogswell), and a Christian minister (Gallaudet) working together on the same mission![31] These three leaders have established a productive model of cooperation for us today as we face a totally new era. They brought together the strengths of three different perspectives (Deaf, hearing parent of Deaf child, hearing) for the common benefit of Deaf children.

The Episcopal Church took the lead in including Deaf congregants in the larger community of faith. Gallaudet's oldest son, Thomas, began a Bible study class for the Deaf in 1850 at St. Stephens Church in New York City. He founded the first church exclusively for the Deaf, St. Ann's Church. He also encouraged a young Deaf man named Henry Syle to pursue ordination. Henry became the first ordained Deaf priest in 1883.[32]

In 1873, the Lutheran Christian Friend's Society established an orphanage near Detroit, Michigan, whose first director, Reverend George Speckhardt, had been a teacher for the Deaf in Germany. Under his leadership, the orphanage reorganized as the Lutheran Institute for the Deaf. One of the school's graduates, Edward Pahl, along with Reverend Augustus Reinke from Chicago, started congregational ministry with Deaf people in March of 1894. Within two years, ministry was occurring in a number of Midwestern cities. The Lutheran denomination adopted Deaf ministry as part of their mission in 1896 and within six months, four full-time ministers were reaching out to the Deaf community.[33]

The Reverend Jacob M. Koehler, a Protestant Episcopal priest who was Deaf, founded the Pennsylvania School for the Deaf in 1883. He was also the pastor of the All Soul's Church for the Deaf in Philadelphia.[34] The Reverend Thomas B. Berry founded the South Dakota Deaf School in 1880.[35] There were at least twenty-eight Deaf clergy ordained to the ministry before World War I and almost another fifty ordained Deaf ministers by 1981 when "Deaf History: A Narrative History of Deaf America" was published. The vast majority of Deaf clergy at the dawn of the 20th Century were Episcopalians. Today, there is a dramatic decrease of clergy and virtual disappearance of Deaf ministry within the Episcopal Church. It would be interesting to explore the causes of this change. Is this decline possibly one of the fallouts of the 1880 Congress of Milan? Did the next generation of Deaf adults during the early 1900's grow up Deaf-Oral and lose their connection with the Deaf-World and linguistic competency? Was this the root cause of a crisis of faith in the Deaf community during the first part of the 20th Century?[36]

In the same way that the African-American church was the place for maintaining cultural connections and identity, the Deaf church and Deaf ministries kept American Sign Language (ASL) very much alive through the darkest days of Oralism. The church was not a leader in the fight for maintaining sign language in the instruction of children and in a few instances may have been oppressive, but it was generally a place where Deaf people could gather and express themselves in their native language freely and without fear. It was a place of welcome for all Deaf whether connected with a residential school or not. Whether to use manual sign language or not was never an issue in the church; Deaf worship and Bible study always involved signing. There is generally a stronger presence of ASL in Deaf churches than in Deaf ministries of hearing churches throughout the last 125 years, but manual sign language has been the clearly preferred method of expressing the gospel and bringing people together for fellowship.

There has existed an argument that Christianity was imposed on the Deaf community by the hearing community; it is viewed as the faith of the oppressor. This perspective loses validity when this logic is applied to other communities. Every cultural group that has been greatly influenced by Christianity was at one time pre-Christian. Rome was not always Roman Catholic. England was not always Anglican. Christianity is a religion of conversion. Even a child who grows up in a Christian home must *become* a Christian to *be* a Christian. The point made here is that Christianity has been the historic faith of the Deaf community largely because of a healthy philosophy in the intrinsic value of each individual. Deafness is not a curse as primitive religions may believe. Deafness is not a disability as the scientific community maintains. From the Christian perspective, God does not make mistakes. Deafness is a part of one's creation by a perfect God who is full of love for His handiwork. Our Judeo-Christian heritage views the individual as a beautiful creation of God who is called into a personal relationship with the Creator. Virtually every Deaf church and Deaf ministry (and in many hearing churches) the Deaf community has been recognized as a distinct language and cultural group.

As is critical in the maintaining of the other cultural groups mentioned, religious faith is a vital part of one's ability to maintain cultural identity as a dispersed people. A loss of religious faith results in the devastation of cultural identity. One of my favorite sayings is *"Created Deaf in the Image of God!"*[37] It is important to realize that one is created in the image of God and called for God's purposes on earth. Deaf people have the same right as any people group in the world to explore spiritual issues and have an experience of personal faith. This is what gives people hope; individually and collectively. Deaf individuals have the right to discover themselves as people created to experience relationship with their Creator that is uniquely theirs to share with others who are Deaf.

Personal Narrative ———————————————— Chad Entinger

The Deaf community is a scattered population. Deaf people are not concentrated in one specific geographic area; they are scattered and live all over the world.

I have asked hearing children to name different countries around the world. Answers have included China, Austria, Afghanistan, Russia, and Canada, among others. I remember one four year-old boy answered, "Texas!"

My point in asking children to name different countries is that deaf people live in each of these countries. If I were to ask you to show me a specific country flag that would represent deaf people as a whole, the correct answer would be to show me every flag that exists for all countries around the world because deaf people live in each of those countries.

Hence ministry to this scattered population is extremely difficult. It would not be like having a Chinese ministry and going to China to reach Chinese people. There are deaf people living in China. But, as has been said, deaf people live in other countries as well (including Texas!).

This is an incredibly exciting time to reach out to the Deaf community, particularly the children and youth. They deserve the same opportunities as their hearing peers to develop their sense of spiritual life. We want to be positive role models for teens in our lifestyles, relationships, and personal faith. Deaf teens need to be presented opportunities to question, struggle, and be "transformed by the renewing of their minds" (Romans 12:2) without external pressures to conform.

Our goal should be to present clear information about a personal relationship with God through Jesus Christ in their language; and without hindrance of dogma or denominational doctrine. Ministry to the Deaf community is not about numbers. It seems that often at conferences for hearing people, there are hundreds, even thousands of attendees. Do not expect this (although it would be great!) when focusing specifically on Deaf ministry. This is the reality of the Diaspora. Expect that the Deaf person you know WILL come to know Jesus. Knowing a few, or even only ONE, Deaf person is enough to begin the process of reaching out to others.

Jesus would agree with that last statement. He talked about the importance of ONE in Luke 15. A whole chapter was used to share three parables that all carry the same theme! The shepherd who found his lost sheep, the woman who found her lost coin, and the father whose lost son came back home all rejoiced over ONE! This is enough evidence to prove that Jesus rejoices over one. Often it takes a dozen, thirty, or 100 before we, as humans, rejoice.

Yes, ministry to Deaf people, a scattered population, is extremely difficult and requires excellence and consistency. Seems like quite a challenge, doesn't it? Are you up to the task?

Discussion and Review

Deaf DIASPORA
Chapter 1—Scattered Community

Expressions

Share about your cultural background. What are some of your cultural influences? What do you see as other cultural traits you may have?

Challenge

Define enculturation and acculturation. Give one example of each.

What can be learned from the four examples of Diaspora? Have you ever personally experienced a Diaspora? Explain.

Describe the results of the Diaspora by each group. Summarize what can be learned by the experience of each group. Which one serves as the most beneficial model for the Deaf community to emulate?

What is the spiritual legacy of each group? How does the spiritual faith of a culture influence the viability and sustainability of that culture?

In your opinion, how important are the various aspects of cultural identity mentioned: language, values, homeland, and spiritual connections.

Scripture

"My eyes will watch over them for their good, and I will bring them back to this land. I will build them up and not tear them down; I will plant them and not uproot them. I will give them a heart to know me, that I am the LORD. They will be my people, and I will be their God, for they will return to me with all their heart."
Jeremiah 24:6-7

Do you believe this Scripture applies to any culture and society or just to the Jewish nation? Explain your reasoning. How might this apply to Deaf-World?

Application

How would you describe the primary challenges of a ministry to members of a community in Diaspora?

What is the practical application to Deaf ministry?

Chapter 2—Changes in Deaf-World

The Deaf community has a proud heritage and legacy. It is vital to understand the importance of Deaf culture in the lives of Deaf people.

The Baby Boomers

The year was 1964. The country was in turmoil. The United States was bogged down in the Vietnam War abroad and dramatic change was occurring domestically. Martin Luther King, Jr. was thirty-five years old and had won the Nobel Peace Prize. President Lyndon Johnson just signed the Civil Rights Act of 1964 and was preparing to sign the Voting Rights Act of 1965. Woodstock was still five years away and America was already entering into frightening changes in acceptable standards for sexual morality and behavior.

There also was something else making a significant impact in the lives of many Americans; a virus known as the German measles. Also known as the Rubella epidemic, this mild childhood illness has a dramatic affect on an unborn baby, if the mother contracts the measles while pregnant. The result was more than 20,000 babies born with various birth defects. People born during this time who were affected by the measles are commonly referred to as the Rubella babies. A large number of these children were born deaf. A vaccine for Rubella became available in 1969. Children have been routinely vaccinated since then which helps prevent the spread of the measles. The net result for the Deaf community was a dramatic increase in the numbers of deaf and hard of hearing children born between 1964 and 1969.[38]

In the middle of the 1970s, when the front line of the Rubella babies was approaching later elementary school, two laws were passed on the federal level that would prove to have a significant impact on the Deaf community: Section 504 of the Rehabilitation Act of 1973 and "Public Law 94-142" in 1975 (later renamed the Individuals with Disabilities Education Act—IDEA). Essentially, these laws required school systems to provide a free and appropriate education to children with disabilities, including those who are deaf. The key factor impacting the cultural landscape of the Deaf-World is the requirement that children be educated in the "Least Restrictive Environment." Simply stated, residential schools are viewed by most educators and parents as a more restrictive environment than the mainstream educational setting. Many in the Deaf-World take the opposite position. They maintain that the least restrictive environment is the one with total access to communication—the residential schools.[39] Students at schools for the Deaf have direct access to information and do not have to have information filtered through an interpreter. This is a dramatic example of the clash between the hearing and Deaf cultures with regards to divergent views of the proper education of Deaf and hard of hearing children.

This bulge of Deaf children filled the residential schools to capacity. These young people would graduate from high school between 1982 and 1987. It is significant to note that the pinnacle of Deaf-pride occurred in 1988, at a time when the Deaf baby boomers were young adults and many were in college. The landmark event was the "Gallaudet Revolution" or a movement more popularly known as "Deaf President Now!" It was a remarkably well-managed statement of Deaf autonomy and strength. A worldwide celebration of Deaf culture called "The Deaf Way" occurred the following year, 1989.[40] The energy and vision of this generation is tremendous and exciting. At the same time, there was a major shift nationally towards establishing Deaf education programs in local school districts known as educational mainstreaming. The least restrictive environment was being determined by officials to be local school districts where students would compete more directly with their hearing peers. This would prove to be of great significance to the future of Deaf-World.

Membership in the Deaf-World

Dr. Harlan Lane, a leading scholar in the field of deafness describes the debate between those who view "deafness-as-disability" and those who understand "deafness-as-culture." He labels this the "infirmity model" verses the "cultural model."[41] Without a doubt, this continues to be a defining (and troubling) issue. Some define a Deaf person viewed as being "hearing impaired" (a pathological or medical perspective) or while others prefer "Deaf/Hard of hearing" (a cultural perspective). Lane has written extensively about the devastation that this "infirmity model" has wrecked on Deaf individuals and the community at large.

Dr. Lane, along with Dr. Ben Bahan[42] and Dr. Robert Hoffmeister[43] in the book *A Journey into DEAF-WORLD* describe the primary aspects of Deaf culture including the language (ASL), "common mores and values"[44] and "other bonding forces in Deaf culture, namely its athletic, social, and political organizations, and its artistic expression."[45] The authors describe the "unifying force of shared oppression"[46] from the hearing world. Mores (*pronounced "more'-ays"*) define acceptable ways of social interaction and customs. Common mores clearly applies to the Deaf culture. One example is the desire to be included in conversations and addressed directly. The concept of common values is more suspect; meaning, to describe Deaf people as having common values is inaccurate. This certainly does not apply to the arena of personal morality so there may be some disagreement as to the meaning of the word, "values." At best, this is a slippery statement. There is a value on being treated with respect, not pity, but it could be argued that this is a more general human value. A saying that has undergone various forms over the years basically states that Deaf people can do anything hearing people can do, other than hear. Implied in this adage is there is equal diversity among Deaf people as hearing people, eliminating specific *Deaf* values. Common mores is the more accurate description of the Deaf culture. The Deaf community is quite diverse (more so than ever before) and this diversity may be more perceived by some as a threat to the Deaf way of life. The authors express concern over the potentially fragmenting force of "diversity."[47]

The "land of the Deaf"[48] is in "the network of residential schools for the Deaf, which are the foundation of the DEAF-WORLD in the U.S., as in many other lands."[49] The authors continue, "The DEAF-WORLD favors voluntary separation for Deaf children in residential schools and is bitterly opposed to mainstreaming most Deaf children in local hearing schools."[50] This is a broad generalization of Deaf perspective and may be an acceptable generalization for the previous Deaf generation but not necessarily so for the next generation. Without a doubt, the socialization available in the residential schools is passionately desired by many young people whether the educational setting is or not. The athletic, social, political organizations and artistic expression are a significant part of Deaf-World. There is great interest in sports (particularly any involving Deaf athletes) and changing interest in social and political organizations. This was one of the ways that Deaf people made new friends, through athletic competitions between schools for the Deaf. Most older Deaf people have very fond memories of their residential schools.

The Deaf community has a distinctive culture and historic legacy. One of the landmark works on Deaf history is Dr. Jack Gannon's *Deaf Heritage: A Narrative History of Deaf America* published in 1981 by the National Association of the Deaf. Although published before all the changes mentioned in this book, it chronicles the proud history of the Deaf community. He wrote a second book in 1989, *When the World Heard Gallaudet* about the "Deaf President Now!" movement in 1988. In the Christian market, DeAnn Sampley published a book in 1989 entitled, *A Guide to Deaf Ministry: Let's Sign Worthy of the Lord* published by

Zondervan. Sampley's book has a strong Deaf cultural focus and was a good ministry resource for that era.[51]

Another interesting insight into the cultural priorities of the Deaf-World is an informal list of the "Seven Deadly Deaf Sins" written by Barry Strassler, the Editor of DeafDigest. This list is an indication of the sensitivities of those within the Deaf culture. His list includes:

- Sin #1—Parents deciding what is best for their deaf child
- Sin #2—To pull a deaf child out of a group of same-age deaf friends in order to mingle solely with the hearing kids
- Sin #3—Telling a deaf child sign language is bad
- Sin #4—Denying one's deafness
- Sin #5—Using the TV set as deaf child's babysitter
- Sin #6—Overprotecting a deaf child
- Sin #7—constantly criticizing deaf child's speech, implying that other deaf children speak "better"[52]

The Deaf community has a tradition of tolerance for individual communication preferences. In a twist of irony, those who draw strict lines around what it REALLY means to be "Deaf" are breaking with the Deaf tradition of inclusiveness. The historic Deaf community is amazingly accepting of people who are different whether by birth, race, disability, communication style, or personality. An individual may have progressive hearing loss (happens over years) and later that person becomes adopted into the community and culture. Hearing children of Deaf adults certainly have a special place within Deaf-World although many experience a sense of being outsiders, as people caught between two worlds. There has historically been a desire within the Deaf community to build meaningful relationships with those who are willing to be true friends. Deaf people have generally experience enough discrimination and separation therefore they have little tolerance for cutting-off others based on perceived differences. The key desirable traits for friendship in Deaf-World are authenticity, a willingness to treat people as equals, and an avoidance of trying to control the Deaf person. This has historically been a universal and fundamental value within Deaf-World.

Mainstreaming in public schools

The mainstreaming movement in the public schools has been the single most significant factor in creating the Deaf Diaspora. At the same time, it is short-sighted to view mainstreaming solely as a threat to the Deaf way of life. If we take the isolationist posture of clinging to a proud past, we ignore the potential benefits of the new culture being created. Both Deaf children and our public schools have adapted fairly well to this new model of education. Public schools offer a continuum of services from a self-contained class to full inclusion in the regular classroom with the benefit of a sign language interpreter and possibly a resource teacher. The primary problem for the Diaspora in the mainstreamed setting comes from a common experience of social isolation, including separation from Deaf peers. Students seem to do fairly well academically, particularly when it comes to developing literacy skills.

As one example of this shift towards mainstreaming, in the school year 2002-2003, there were 128 Deaf and hard of hearing children, in Kindergarten through 12th grade, in Jefferson County Public Schools in Louisville, Kentucky—a metro area of just over one million people. Only eight of these children attended the school for the Deaf that is roughly an hour-and-a-half away while 120 were mainstreamed. This is equivalent to one child in fifteen attending the school for the Deaf. Twenty-six of these mainstreamed children are kindergarten age or younger and attend the Louisville Deaf Oral School. Seventy-two of the mainstreamed children are Deaf/Oral and only forty-eight uses "Total Communication" which means some level of proficiency in manual sign language. This means sixty percent do not sign at all. Only four of ten use some form of manually signed language. Thirty-nine of these students are in seven schools and there are a total of fifty-five students scattered across the rest of the system in eighteen different locations. Many of these students are the only Deaf person in their school. Very few are fluent in American Sign Language. Another disturbing percentage that represents the changes that are occurring in Deaf-World is that forty-two percent of the students in Kindergarten or younger have cochlear implants—a very controversial issue in the Deaf-World—while only fourteen percent of the children in first grade or above have the implant. In other words, almost half of the children under six years old had received a cochlear implant, revealing a dramatic increase over previous years.

There is much debate regarding the actual impact of the mainstreamed educational setting on the overall education of Deaf students. Experts disagree as to the best way to teach reading skills to people for whom English is a second language. There is even debate as to the importance of Deaf role models in the educational setting. Advocates of Deaf culture are puzzled as to why this would even be a question. Of course, Deaf children need adult Deaf role models. Many hearing educators seem to have an underlying fear of connecting Deaf students with Deaf adults who value English differently from the hearing majority. There is debate as to the proper role of American Sign Language in the development of language skills and literacy. Regardless of ones perspective of the mainstreamed educational settings, this educational shift has been rapid and significant.

The speed of change has created cultural vertigo that threw virtually everyone in Deaf-World off balance. The education of Deaf children in the mainstreamed setting has not been nearly as devastating as initially feared by many in the Deaf-World. At the same time, the mainstreamed school setting does have many drawbacks and barriers; regardless of the promises of the public school educators and specialists. The reality is that the future holds no real prospect of returning to an earlier day. According to commonly accepted estimates, four-out-of-five Deaf children in our country are being educated in the mainstream setting. Thirty years ago, it was one-out-of-five. This is a dramatic change in the environment of the next generation of the Deaf community.

The Explosion of Technology

Technology is a critical new factor in the lives of this new generation of Deaf people. Technology is improving dramatically for making mainstreaming a viable option but lags behind the needs of the Deaf. The most dramatic changes have occurred more recently but all this rapid infusion of technology began during the late 1980s. Personal computers complete with word processing capability (including spelling and grammatical checks) make success in the mainstreamed classroom more possible. The whole computer-related industry is attractive to people who process information visually. Many Deaf students excel in the areas of computer programming, CAD (computer assisted design), and web design. Although there is plenty of room to improve, more classrooms are using captioned videos, subtitled DVDs and more visual formats.

Deaf children and youth have access to new and exciting technology that connects them with their families and each other. The 2-way pager is informally called the "Cell Phone of the Deaf" because it facilitates direct communication. "Instant Messaging" and "Chat Rooms" are ways to communicate on the Internet. Newer pagers allow for this conversation to occur through wireless connections. The TTY (teletypewriter), many times referred to as a TDD (Telecommunications Device for the Deaf), is now almost obsolete in this generation. Because of high speed access, personal computers and web cams, Deaf people can now communicate visually with each other over long distances. There are also relay services on-line that allow you to sign to an operator who will speak for you to a third party. A whole new language of abbreviations for faster communication has emerged. A few common examples are LMK—"let me know," CU—"see you later," and BRB—"be right back." The list seems endless and is actually creating a third language for youth; one that includes both Deaf and hearing teenagers!

There seems to be a difference in perception between the generations of Deaf people regarding the positive or negative impact of technology. There is a common opinion among older Deaf people that technology has isolated people within the Deaf community by keeping younger Deaf at home in front of computer screens or subtitled DVD movies. Technology removes the incentive of getting out and socializing with others. The younger people tend to see this same technology as a gateway into relationships through instant messaging, video relays, and emails.

The impact of medical technology is an emotional debate. Most recently this debate surrounds the concept of surgery on Deaf children for cochlear implants. The next controversy on the horizon will possibly be the impact of stem cell research on preventing deafness. The whole concept of "fixing" children born with limited hearing is offensive and perceived as a threat to many in the Deaf-World. There is no way to foresee the future but we can predict that technology will continue to rapidly change the world of deafness. It does not change our cultural view of Deafness but it certainly alters the variables in the discussion. We are in the midst of unparalleled change in our world as a result of technology. This technology has a direct impact on Deaf-World. There are new opportunities and accessibility; there are also new dangers. Regardless of the pros and cons, technology is a constant and daily reality in the lives of Deaf individuals. It continues to create rapid change in Deaf-World.

Rise of Secular Academic Perspective

Another dramatic change over the past forty years has been the secularization of public education in our country. In 1962, The U.S. Supreme Court declared it unconstitutional to include state-sponsored school prayer as part of instruction in the public school setting. This does not forbid prayer in schools but requires that they are not state-sponsored nor part of the instructional day. There are other Supreme Court decisions, Federal and State laws, and local school system decisions that have continued to change the culture of the public education institutions and their perspective on the role of religion in the schools. Many times, the proverbial baby has been thrown out with the bathwater. The school administration seems uncertain about the legality of Christian organizations being on campus. Churches may overreact and totally avoid involvement with public education. At times, this secularization provides a platform for those with clearly anti-Christian perspectives to proclaim their worldviews as authoritative. As a society, we often fall prey to the guardians of political correctness. People in public school systems become afraid to express their personal perspectives especially if they tend to be more traditional or conservative.

The Deaf community has also been directly affected by these larger cultural changes. Historically, religious instruction was viewed as part of raising well-adjusted Deaf children in the residential setting. In today's world, there is little or no formal religious instruction on either the residential or the mainstreamed school campuses. There is great sensitivity within the Deaf culture about hearing people trying to control or oppress Deaf people. This perspective has been generalized to the role of the church in the Deaf experience. The church may be viewed as manipulative of Deaf individuals in an effort to *save their souls*. The clear tendency over the past two decades is to view the Christian faith in a negative light, as being detrimental to Deaf individuals and culture. There are surely examples of oppression within church history but this is basically a false characterization of the actual influence of the church in Deaf-World as was discussed in the first chapter.

In the hearing world, there is diversity of educational perspectives and institutions; from Ivy League schools to private colleges, state universities, Christian colleges and denominational seminaries. This myriad of schools presents a variety of perspectives and philosophical approaches to everything from history to psychology to physics to religion. In Deaf-World, there is basically one research institution that specializes in education of Deaf students, Gallaudet University. What is missing is a healthy balance of multiple perspectives, especially those from a Christian point of view. Without other strong educational institutions to create academic balance, much is accepted without question, which hinders healthy dissent and debate. The preponderance of academic literature has been from a completely secular worldview. There is a need for greater Christian scholarship in the academic world as it relates to the field of deafness.

Changes in Education and Traditional Worksites

There has been a significant shift in the type of education received by most Deaf students at the secondary level. Most Deaf education now directs students towards college and includes little vocational training. The move away from vocational training is having an adverse effect on the employability of many academically average or below average students. The good news is that more Deaf high school graduates are entering (and completing) college than ever before; the bad news is that unemployment among the Deaf, even those with college degrees, is unusually high. There may be opportunities for employment in the skilled trades that are ignored for lack of vocational training. A high level of unemployment is another isolating factor that scatters the Deaf community.

Historically, a large percentage of the Deaf community worked in relatively few trades. The post office, printing companies, factories, shipping companies (handling of packages) and manufacturing companies hired many Deaf employees. Many of these companies, including the post office, have become more automated and therefore have fewer job opportunities. The result is a reduction in the overall number of employees and the loss of jobs by many Deaf individuals. Traditionally, the workplace was one of the places for meeting and socializing with other Deaf people. For the most part, this is no longer the case. The scattering of job opportunities is one of the contributors to the Deaf Diaspora.

In the current day, there is concern in educational circles as to the impact the 2003 Elementary and Secondary Education Act, known as *No Child Left Behind.* This is particularly a concern regarding the education of children with special needs including those who are overcoming communication barriers. It may contain positive aspects for increasing pressure on Deaf students to perform at levels competitive with their hearing peers. Not all students can develop the reading competency necessary to succeed in college. In the past, vocational training led many young Deaf people to careers, while now the focus on training for college may actually have the result of leaving some children behind who could otherwise succeed.

Loss of Deaf Christian role models

A common phrase in the Christian community is "faith is caught, not taught." We become people who believe in Jesus by being with people who know and follow Him. Christian role models are a vital part of faith development. Because of the secularization of our society in general, and the "baby boomers" of the Deaf community in specific, there has been a significant loss in the availability of Deaf Christian role models, especially young adults, who have the most direct influence on Deaf children and youth.

In a workshop setting, I may ask the older Deaf people in the room about the Christian Deaf role models they remember from their childhood. Essentially, each one says the same thing, "Many, many strong Christians influenced me." Then, I ask the participants under thirty-years old the same question. Very rarely can someone name even one Deaf person who influenced them spiritually. One young woman, who reflects the common experience of her generation, referred to a couple of hearing people in her church who helped her understand God's love but she knew no other Deaf Christians. This is a dramatic (and frightening) change over three generations in the Deaf culture. An important part of developing a real and dynamic faith is having people, who experience life like you do, who have committed their lives to Christ. This is not a "hearing" religion; it is a personal relationship between the Creator and the creation.

Like many great booms, a bust usually follows. This is part of why the change was so rapid. A vacuum was left behind as the Deaf Baby Boomers grew up and moved on. This was a huge hit on the Deaf community. There was the impact of the state and federal laws which led to mainstreaming leaving large areas of residential school campuses were unused or under-used. Residential schools are losing students to local school districts. Finding an adequate number and quality of sign language interpreters has become a huge challenge. Sometimes Deaf students are in educational settings without any interpreter at all. With mainstreaming came a renewed focus on Signed English and speech-reading/verbal skills for students and loss of competency in ASL and disconnect with Deaf culture and community. It has created a Deaf cultural crisis.

When you think about this world-shattering change, remember that most of this cultural transformation occurred during the last decade of the 20th century. In ten short years, the entire world of the Deaf community went from the mountaintop to the valley; from a wave of Deaf Pride to a struggle for their very existence as an identifiable people group. Enculturation was rapidly giving way to extreme acculturation by the majority culture. This has been a culture shock[53] for an entire people group.

[Jesus] replied, "You know the saying, `Red sky at night means fair weather tomorrow, red sky in the morning means foul weather all day.' You are good at reading the weather signs in the sky, but you can't read the obvious signs of the times!" (Matthew 16:2-3, NLT). The coming storm will water our fields because we have irrigated properly and built dams in the right places; or we will be washed away by the wind and water. We must be intentional and consistent in our response to the Deaf Diaspora. To have effective ministry requires reading the signs of the times.

❧❧❧

Personal Narrative————————————————————Chad Entinger

"I'm Deaf."

This is what I signed, among many others things, to an audience. After I was finished speaking and most of the audience had left, I made my way to a telephone. I proceeded to make a call and put the phone to my ear and mouth. After talking, literally, on the phone and hanging up, a Deaf lady, who happened to see me talking on the phone, walked up to me.

"You're NOT Deaf!" she signed, "You can hear a little bit and talk on the phone. If you can do those things, then you are hard of hearing. You're NOT Deaf!"

Fast forward a few months.

"I'm hard of hearing." I signed these words to a different audience. Immediately a Deaf woman stopped me upon seeing me sign these words.

"You're NOT hard of hearing!" she signed, "You're DEAF! You're Deaf! It doesn't matter how much hearing you have lost or if you can hear just a little bit, you're Deaf, not hard of hearing!"

Utter chaos!

Deaf? Hard of hearing?

Which one am I?

Audiologists would label me as both! I'm literally Deaf in my left ear and hard of hearing in my right ear.

Utter chaos!

Deaf? Hard of hearing?

Anthropologists (cultural) would label me as both! When they see me around Deaf people, they would label me as Deaf, courtesy of my sign language skills and cultural mannerisms. If they were to see me around hearing people, they would label me as hard of hearing (or some would dare call me hearing impaired!). This label would come as a result of seeing me use my voice as I interact with hearing people.

Utter chaos!

Deaf? Hard of hearing?

God would label me as neither! I am physically Deaf and I know that God made me that way. Though, God knows full well that I am not spiritually "Deaf."

I'm relieved!

The sense of what it means to be Deaf is being completely redefined for a number of reasons.

If you were to take a survey of various types of Deaf people and ask them, "What does it mean to be Deaf?" Here are some of common responses.

"I use sign language."

"It means I have a hearing loss. I can still act and be like hearing people."

"I am part of a different and distinct cultural group."

"It doesn't always mean using sign language. I don't know how to sign. I'm oral."

Seems like utter chaos within a people group?

With a majority of deaf children being raised by hearing parents (more than 90%) and mainstreamed in public schools, fewer are exposed to the "Deaf Culture." And while the pathologically-minded and culturally-minded people wage war, the sense of what it means to be Deaf is being redefined—it feels like a culture fading away.

Some people argue that the Deaf Culture is vanishing, while others disagree. One thing, though, that is of no argument: Deaf people are vanishing to hell every day. Doesn't that just make you cringe?

Discussion and Review

Deaf DIASPORA
Chapter 2—Changes in Deaf-World

Expressions

Describe some of the major changes you have seen in society during your lifetime.

Challenge

Describe some basic differences between the pathological and cultural perspectives of deafness.

What are some of the ways the experiences of the Deaf "Baby Boomers" paralleled the post-World War II baby boom in the general population?

Educational mainstreaming and technology are identified as two primary factors in creating the Diaspora. Why is this so?

What does it mean to be part of the Deaf culture? Contrast earlier definitions of membership in the Deaf community with the changes that seem to be occurring.

Scripture

[Jesus] replied, "You know the saying, 'Red sky at night means fair weather tomorrow, red sky in the morning means foul weather all day.' You are good at reading the weather signs in the sky, but you can't read the obvious signs of the times!" (Matthew 16:2-3)

What kinds of warnings are on the horizon for Deaf ministry? What happens if we ignore the changes that have occurred?

Application

This book is introducing a fairly radical departure in the definition of Deaf culture from literature published during the 1980s and 1990s. How will you respond to others who hold a different view of deafness? In ministry, why is it important to understand these various perspectives?

Chapter 3—Crisis REAL

The Christian faith is always just one generation away from extinction.

"What? NO WAY!"

His puzzlement was real.

Here was a very bright sixteen year old young man, who had been Deaf since his early years, who was totally baffled by my comment that God can understand the beautiful language of American Sign Language (ASL).

He signed emphatically, "God doesn't know sign language! He is a Hearing God! God cannot understand my signs!"

Like most Deaf people, he was the only Deaf person in his family. Although his parents dragged him to church for his entire life, he still made little or no sense out of the gospel.

I assured him that God both signs and reads sign language with incredible skill. God knows his thoughts, feelings, experiences and loves him completely. God is the creator of everything and the author of all languages and cultures. I explained, in sign language, that God wants a personal relationship with him through Jesus Christ.

He needed some time to figure all this out. The gospel made sense to him at some point because he later became a leader in his church. He experienced the grace and love of God and wanted to share this with others. But first, he had to make sense out of a "hearing" God who knew his language and understood his Deaf heart.

Unfortunately, this is not the only time I have witnessed this confusion. How in the world did we come to the point that this teenager, and many other Deaf and hard of hearing adolescents, would be completely oblivious to the fact that the Creator also wants a personal relationship with His Creation?

We have been watching a crisis of huge proportion unfold before our very eyes over the last two decades of the 20th Century. The Christian faith has become almost completely extinguished from the Deaf experience. This crisis goes virtually unrecognized by the larger Christian body. There is a general assumption in churches that since there are no Deaf "in our church then they must be going somewhere else." The reality is that, by far, most Deaf are going nowhere for worship or Bible study. There is a general disconnect with spiritual things.

If there was a singular issue that serves as the greatest peril, it is the loss of young Deaf Christian role models. Nothing is more devastating to the perpetuation of the Christian faith in Deaf-World than the absence of people who *"look like me, think like me, are Deaf like me, are older than me and love Jesus."* God is blessing us with a revival in Deaf-World among young Deaf adults and Deaf teenagers. We must do everything possible to create an environment where young Deaf people are interacting with Deaf adults who are sincere and mature followers of Jesus Christ.

The Missing Generation

In the years following World War I—known as the Great War or the War to End All Wars—there was a huge emotional and spiritual vacuum left by the carnage that many young Americans and Brits witnessed and experienced. The war was commonly referred to as the "War of the Trenches" because of the great amount of time spent fighting between long muddy ditches, encompassed by barbed wire. A generation of idealistic, well-educated young people found themselves stuck in Europe in these ditches of death. These young veterans became known as the "Lost Generation." Their pre-war illusions of grandeur quickly dissolved into the gloomy disillusionment of the horrors of war.

The generation of Deaf who were born in the 1960s and 1970s are the best educated, most enlightened group of Deaf people the world has ever known. They rose through the ranks of society during a time of unparalleled opportunity and Deaf pride. There was little that could stop them. Yet, as they became adults, many of their support systems dissolved and scattered. For the most part, there was no spiritual foundation for them to lean on; a spiritual barrenness previously unknown in the Deaf community.

There is a missing generation of Christian Deaf young adults. We stand at the precipice of a completely secularized Deaf culture. By far, most people who come to faith do so by the end of their high school career. People may stray and explore other ideas during the young adult years but they have a foundation upon which to return. Proverbs teaches, *"Train up a child in the way he should go; even when he is old, he will not depart from it."* (Proverbs 22:6, NLT)

There is little empirical data to document the spiritual condition of people. This premise is based on observations and conversations. There is an eerie absence of Deaf people under forty-five years old in church. Ask anyone who is involved with Deaf ministry. Many Deaf ministries have become ghost towns for almost two generations; many ministries and churches have actually closed. This generation experiences the greatest secular opportunities in history but is mostly disconnected with personal faith and involvement in the local church. Ask anyone who interprets in a hearing church about the number and ages of Deaf who attend regularly. You will be shocked. During a one-week period, I had an email from a Deaf Baptist minister and a personal conversation with the Roman Catholic priest with the Deaf who made similar observations, *"Where are all the young people? They are not in our churches."*

Has this missing generation of Deaf young adults infiltrated the "hearing church?" No. They are not present. Are they connected with para-church organizations like Youth For Christ, Intervarsity or Young Life? No. Have they joined other religions and become followers of other faiths? No. They have simply decided that God is a "hearing God" who doesn't make sense to them. They have enough integrity to avoid pretending they believe.

Most hearing churches do not have a Deaf ministry even those *with* sign language interpreters. There is a huge difference between ministry and providing interpreted services. Ministry involves relationships and investing one's life into another person. Providing interpreted worship services is important but is no substitute for authentic Deaf worship and consistent relational ministry.

No matter how large a church is, it is still limited by geography, denomination and general perception by the community. One of the most exciting "seeker model" churches based on the "Purpose-driven Church"[54] has over a dozen skilled sign language interpreters for their services. They have a regular Deaf Bible study and fellowships. They are very intentional about reaching out to the Deaf community. Still, there are relatively few Deaf members under forty years old and until recently, essentially no Deaf children or youth actively involved. There are some Deaf churches that are applying the seeker model and seeing promising results. There is also a ministry to Deaf young adults that is spreading across the country named Deaf Café based on this model. It could be described as a "Purpose-Driven Deaf Club." These are all efforts to reach out to a generation of Deaf who are generally disconnected from the Christian faith.

In the past, one place the Deaf community would gather was at church. This is no longer true. Schools used to promote our Judeo-Christian heritage as part of becoming a mature adult. Now, Christianity is viewed as suspect. Deaf culture used to be a clearly defined community connected with the residential schools which included religious instruction. Now, the vast majority of Deaf children and youth are in secular mainstreamed settings. Once, the Deaf community was rich with Christian role models who shared the faith with the next generation. Now, there are almost two full generations of Deaf people with little connection with spiritual things.

Weakening of Moral Values

Many who grew up in the 1960s and 1970s may have known the moral code taught in the Bible but chose to reject it. Many born in the 1980s were never even exposed to it. Imagine growing up without understanding the reasoning behind morality. It is not enough just to conform to the rules of one's parents and ancestors. There must be a practical application to today's challenges and temptations. In one of our GROWgroup Bible studies for Deaf teenagers, the Ten Commandments were discussed. One of the high school students in attendance gave a puzzled response, *"Ten Commandments? What's that?"* She had attended church with her family on-and-off over the years and had missed one of the fundamentals of the Judeo-Christian heritage. She is not unlike many of today's young Deaf people; she was unfamiliar with even the basics of the Christian faith.

Most people are keenly aware of the abandonment of traditional moral values in our country during the last quarter of the 20th Century, the so-called "Sexual Revolution." The Deaf community is not immune to these changes. I remember a conversation with a well-known Deaf Christian minister in 1986. He was lamenting the incredible increase in immoral behavior of young Deaf college students. He was shocked at the level of sexual promiscuity and had some very real concerns about many of the students. Along with many of the "Deaf Rights" that developed during the 1980s and 1990s was an increased sense of the individual right to make moral decisions without any external authority including parents, the Bible and tradition. The Christian traditions of their hearing parents were viewed as oppression by the hearing world.

Homosexuality is a huge and disconcerting issue confronting Deaf-World. Gays and Lesbians have a significant presence in the Deaf and interpreter communities. The Rainbow Alliance of the Deaf was organized in May 1977. They held annual conventions in various locations across the nation until 1985 when they began to meet every other year. They claim over twenty chapters in the U.S. and Canada. There are other homosexual organizations that specifically target Deaf youth.[55] The national interpreter certification board, the Registry for Interpreters for the Deaf (RID), has a special subgroup for Lesbian and Gay Interpreters and Transliterators (LeGIT). Recently, it was decided this acronym was too exclusive so the proposed name change is BLeGIT—"Bi-Sexual, Lesbian, Gay, Intersexed, and Transgendered" interpreters and transliterators.[56] Development of a healthy sexual identity is even more complicated when one has a communication barrier with his or her parents. This is explored more in-depth in Chapter 8.

There is an array of practical moral issues confronted by Deaf youth. What is right and wrong about homosexual, premarital or extra-marital relations? What about lying, cheating or stealing? Why not kill? Is something wrong if I am never caught? Should we go to war? Why is forgiveness important? Is gossip okay? What's wrong with envy, jealousy or wanting what someone else has? What are the foundational values to build a productive life upon? Facing these issues without the benefit of mature, older Deaf spiritual role models makes it a difficult challenge for the current generation.

It is a crisis of culture.

There is a prevailing bias in the medical and educational communities that deafness is a disability. This perception of deafness influences the families of the Deaf individual as well as the Deaf person himself or herself. This is especially true of those Deaf people who use only speech-reading/verbal skills. The common term for these individuals among the signing Deaf is "Deaf-Oral." There is a personal pride in some Deaf-Oral individuals for not having to use sign language. They feel fortunate for being able to function without sign language and feel no connection with Deaf culture or identity. I remember hearing of a comment from one young Deaf-Oral man who was puzzled by a discussion about the importance of having Deaf role models. In effect, he said, "Why do we need Deaf role models? We just need role models." He did not identify with Deaf people in general or the Deaf culture in particular.

Some young Deaf people have been acculturated to such an extent that many do not refer to themselves as "Deaf" and many prefer the term "hearing impaired" or even just "hearing" but with assistive devices such as hearing aids. A whole generation of Deaf people has emerged that has little or no sense of Deaf history or cultural identity. This is a loss. I believe parents and educators are making a mistake by isolating children from connections with the richness of Deaf-World. Without these cultural connections, a child may perceive herself or himself as handicapped and lower personal expectations. Many of these Deaf-Oral individuals experience persistent exclusion in the hearing world, yet are not enjoying relationships with other Deaf people. They have become people caught between two worlds and connected with neither. They are without sense of their rich, cultural Deaf heritage. Just like Alex Haley's *Roots* was a journey that helped him overcome self-doubt and imposed inferiority, this disconnect with ones identity as a Deaf person may have a devastating impact on the individual. A sense of identity and connection is a vital building block for a meaningful and productive life.

There are other examples of the breakdown in cultural connections. For example, one of the primary sources of Deaf news and information, SILENT NEWS, was founded by Julius and Harriet Wiggins and began publication in 1969. At one point, it had over 12,000 subscribers and was sent to all 50 states and 27 foreign countries. It ceased publication in 2002 after the death (in 2001) of Julius Wiggins. At one time there were three national deaf publications, SILENT NEWS, DEAF-NATION, and NEWSWAVES. Not one of these is still in circulation.

Evidence of the loss of cultural connection is seen in this observation made in 2003 in DEAFDIGEST—an email newsletter with bits of news and information:

> "DEAF THEATRE BECOMING EXTINCT? Right now we have two viable deaf theatrical groups—the National Theatre of the Deaf and the Deaf West. Way back in the eighties we had approximately 35 local deaf theatrical groups. This list seems to have been whittled down to maybe a half dozen groups, and some of them seem to be on shaky grounds. This is sad."[57]

The crisis of culture may have been exacerbated by the strict definitions of Deaf culture that excludes those who think and communicate differently from those defining membership in the Deaf community. A somewhat disparaging remark may be made to describe a Deaf person as "thinking hearing." This means that person has become so acculturated to the customs of the hearing world that he or she processes information like hearing people do. This is not a compliment; quite the opposite. Many in this new generation of Deaf (who think-hearing) are being excluded by self-appointed gatekeepers of what it means to be culturally Deaf. Many of these cultural guardians are hearing people who take a false sense of militant pride in excluding these non-signing and minimally signing Deaf. Deaf and hearing activists and interpreters need to respect the rights of Deaf individuals to decide for themselves their preference along the communication continuum.

It is a crisis of language.

Deaf thought processes are based primarily in visual cues, not verbal memory. Deaf people think visually. Most have not developed language from overhearing spoken conversations of others. Deaf children of Deaf parents can "overhear" sign language and tend to develop language at the same pace and level as their hearing counterparts. This certainly makes sense for people who acquire information by what they see. Even if a person is Deaf-Oral, he or she is not hearing words, so language is processed differently in the brain. It makes learning the English language a second language for all Deaf, not just those who sign. In reality, some form of manually expressed language is natural for Deaf children. God has created Deaf people to express and receive language visually. Because of the Diaspora, it may be more difficult for Deaf people to experience a connection with others who think visually. There is also a breakdown of the quality of ASL in many areas of the country because of the absence of more formal register ASL language role models. Fortunately, there is a higher standard for educational sign language interpreters evolving that will hopefully stabilize this language drift. Unfortunately, these are hearing people (not Deaf language role models) and are not supposed to be in an instructional role. Without good language role models, there is an increased sense of disconnection and loss of standardization of the language.

Many Deaf people now use some form of manually-coded English, commonly referred to as Signed English. This is a sign language that communicates English words and sentences using signs and symbols. For these Deaf individuals, they think in English structures—the language of their families. There is nothing wrong with thinking in English structures but it involves repetitious mental translations between visual images and linear language structures. This can be an exhausting mental translation experience.

Research and observation show the language most naturally fitted to Deaf thought processes is American Sign Language. ASL is a legitimate language complete with grammatical structure, syntax, and vocabulary. ASL allows one to color the conversation with subtle nuances and complex concepts that are not verbally based. Early acquisition of language, particularly sign language by Deaf children, has been shown to be a vital part of developing later competency in overall communication skills including the understanding of English language structure. American Sign Language can accurately be described as the natural language of the Deaf.

English and ASL are both beautiful languages. The difference between ASL and English can be described as the comparison between watching a sunset and hearing one described. ASL is like watching a movie versus reading the book. ASL is art; English is literature. ASL is spatial and English is linear. English offers a beautiful description of the wind; ASL is experiencing the wind itself. Both are important languages that serve the individual well. When Deaf children are able to express themselves naturally and fluently, they develop important aspects of self-esteem and confidence. These are important building blocks for a successful life including the acquisition of fundamental language skills.

The crisis is due in part to the inability or unwillingness of parents and educators to recognize the importance of Deaf children being able to communicate in a language that comes naturally to them. There has been entirely too much division over this issue. Educators and parents need to recognize the natural draw of the Deaf towards the visual world. Being skilled in ASL has been shown to be beneficial for Deaf children in the acquisition of English concepts and language. As a society, we encourage our children to learn additional languages. Yet, there is hesitancy for Deaf-Oral children to be exposed to sign language. Even a child using primarily speech-reading and verbal skills is guaranteed to enjoy learning a beautiful, expressive second language. It is always beneficial to know a second (and third) language. For Deaf children, it will open the door to friendships with thousands of others with common experiences in life.

It is a crisis of relationships.

The "I" word of the previous Deaf generation was "identity." Sadly, the "I" word of the most recent generation of Deaf persons is "isolation." This may lead to another "I" word, "immaturity." There is a crisis of relationships due in large part to the Deaf Diaspora. Previously, in residential schools, older Deaf adults would teach children and youth how to process information, make decisions, express feelings, respect themselves and others, communicate effectively, and solve personal and interpersonal problems. This isolation created through dispersion inhibits proper social and conceptual development.

Most hearing people have the advantage of learning these basic social skills through overhearing conversations by parents or siblings. This informal learning is virtually impossible for Deaf children in hearing families. Learning has to be a specific and focused experience. Most hearing parents of Deaf children lack the signing skills to understand their Deaf child—to express deep emotions, resolve conflicts, converse and instruct them in the nuances of interpersonal relationships skills. Even for families that can sign, modeling relational skills from those who shares in the child's cultural identity and experience (and shares the same values as the family) are vital. Parents need to have relationships with Deaf adults they trust to help guide and influence their children through adolescence. The Diaspora has certainly made this more difficult to achieve.

The family is the most vital building block of our society. We must do everything within our power to strengthen and restore the family. The inability to communicate clearly with one's own children is clearly a problem in the Deaf spiritual experience. In all reality, the percentage of parents skilled in ASL will remain unchanged, possibly even decrease. Children need adults with whom they can discuss the deeper issues of life. They need people who know their language and how their minds work, and can be sensitive to their questions, concerns, and feelings. Unfortunately, this is virtually impossible without the ability to sign.

Information sharing is a significant part of Deaf culture. Technology has many advantages in making this information sharing more readily accessible but the downside is significant. For example, young Deaf adults are much less likely to attend Deaf social events. This rapid sharing of information via email, instant-messaging, 2-way pagers, etc. can lead to rapid and widespread misunderstandings in relationships. There are positive aspects of this level of communication however there is a downside. Negative comments, arguments, gossip, and rumors can move throughout the Deaf community at cyber-speed and be harmful to relationships and reputations. Many older Deaf see technology as a barrier to relationships. One is quoted as saying, *"The more pagers we have the less united we are; the less pagers we have the more close-knit the Deaf Community is."58*

Deaf students in mainstreamed settings may tend to hide behind or be left behind hearing students in the classroom. It is virtually impossible for a main-streamed Deaf student to contribute to a fast-paced discussion through an inter-preter. They are more likely to withdraw from meaningful classroom interactions. There is a delay of information going in both directions. Input to the conversa-tion may come well after the topic has changed. The reaction from the other stu-dents, even if it is polite, tends to discourage further efforts at contributing in class. This often creates a lowering of expectations by the teacher, peers and the student him/herself. The Deaf student learns how to manipulate the system to pass the required classes. There are fewer opportunities for leadership develop-ment than in the traditional residential settings.

The residential schools of today have their fair share of problems with regards to emotional development and relationships. First and foremost, it is not an ade-quate substitution for daily living as part of one's own family. There are some peo-ple within the system who are antagonistic towards the hearing parents of the Deaf student and serve to drive a wedge into the family unity. As a reflection of the larger society, there is not one value system based on our Judeo-Christian her-itage that teaches right and wrong. Students are exposed to a wide range of val-ues that may be in conflict with the Christian faith. Students do not have the luxury of being away from negative relationships during the evening hours unless they are day students that commute to school. Any negative peer influences and relationships continue after school hours and have less supervision in the dormi-tories than in the classroom. Students can become manipulative of adults in an institutional setting in efforts to get attention.

It is a crisis of community.

The hearing world is not totally accessible to the Deaf and there is a common experience of feeling like a second-class citizen in the hearing society. One may feel out-of-step with hearing people with whom they interact. Many Deaf people never experience a sense of personal peace until they discover people who communicate in their language and share a common experience of deafness. The Diaspora has creat-ed a disconnection with the larger Deaf community. Some blame this situation on "audism"—a term coined by those who perceive the universal oppression of Deaf culture by the hearing majority. Audism is the systemic discrimination against Deaf people by those who hear.[59]

There are some common traits in Deaf young adults of this generation that may come from growing up in isolation from other Deaf adults. There is a general absence of Deaf role models in mainstreamed educational settings. There seems to be the development of an *entitlement mentality* (the world owes me something because I am Deaf) that is personally debilitating. There is considerable concern among the older Deaf community about the disincentive for young Deaf adults to work instead of drawing SSI (Supplemental Security Income—a disability funding source).[60] The traditional work settings are disappearing and many able-bodied Deaf are staying home and drawing welfare instead of entering the work force. Although SSI and other financial supports are helpful, there is a danger in creating dependency on the governmental subsidies.

In 1996, when Lane, Hoffmeiser, and Bahan wrote their book about Deaf-World, there were already significant warning signs of the changes occurring in the Deaf community. They seem to recognize that the new generation of Deaf children and youth were not following in the tracks of their predecessors. "Reportedly, membership in Deaf clubs has been dwindling, especially among young people, who are the next generation of Deaf leaders...One frequently cited cause is that mainstreaming of Deaf children in local schools delays Deaf children's acquisition of ASL and Deaf culture."[61]

The reality is that not only is membership in Deaf clubs dwindling, virtually every gathering of Deaf in the country, including Deaf church, is graying, and shrinking in size. Many traditional Deaf clubs and activities are closing down. Even the important sporting leagues and events, that used to draw large numbers of Deaf, have either decreased in size or even ceased to exist. The Alumni Associations are shrinking; the state Associations of the Deaf are less active in the lives of young people. Deaf are more scattered and less united than any time during the last century. As explained in the opening chapter, this all results from the dispersion of the community and the primary reason for the Deaf Diaspora is the mainstreaming of children into local public schools. Based on the definition of Deaf culture developed during the 1980s and 1990s, the traditional Deaf culture is vanishing.

It is a crisis of faith.

The challenge of the Christian faith is to help each generation discover the gospel for themselves in life-changing ways. Abundant life is offered to all but it has to be received. God doesn't have grandchildren. God only has children, who receive grace by faith. Grace is the outstretched arms of forgiveness from a loving, heavenly father who desires a personal relationship with his children. Without that relationship, people continue with the burden and consequences of their own sin. The Deaf community in general has experienced a crisis of faith partially as a result of the Diaspora.

The spiritual crisis within the Deaf community has a variety of components. Before the 1980s, when most of the Deaf community attended residential schools, there was support from a vibrant religious community in the areas surrounding the schools. There were numerous ministries for Deaf young people from a variety of churches and denominations. Sunday Schools were available for Deaf children and youth. Worship experiences and Christian camps were options (sometimes requirements) for virtually every child. Most of the residential schools had Chaplains who provided religious instruction and relational ministry on the school campus.

That day is no more. Some of the residential schools have been closed down. Most of the others have dramatically decreased enrollments. More students who are sent to the residential schools have complex emotional or physical problems. Because most schools send their students home each weekend, there are relatively small numbers of Deaf children and youth in the area where the schools are located. Both the residential and mainstreamed students are scattered across the state. Few churches still offer programs in these local areas because there are fewer children and youth.

In the communities where these scattered children reside, including those who are mainstreamed, there is little or no inclusion in spiritual instruction or experience. *If* their parents take them to church…and *if* their church has an interpreter…*if* the interpreter is skilled in ASL…and *if* the young person pays attention to the interpreter…the Deaf child *still* feels like an outsider observing a "hearing" experience. Imagine attending a church where you do not understand the language or customs. The Deaf person often feels isolated from the Christian experience. They tend to experience faith in the hearing world as an outsider, an observer.

To illustrate my point of why Deaf children and youth cannot be simply plugged in to a traditional church or youth group setting, even with an interpreter, imagine the performance of "Handel's Messiah" for your average Deaf person. The Hallelujah Chorus is boring when one cannot hear, even with an interpreter. Take away the orchestra, the harmonies, the majesty of the beautiful melody, the powerful voices and you are left with an endless repetition of the one sign for "Hallelujah." One can see why many young Deaf people begin thinking that Christianity is a boring, hearing religion. It just does not make sense to them on a deeper level.

The crisis is real and worth restating; the Christian faith has been progressively erased out of the Deaf experience during the last quarter of the 20th Century in America. The Deaf community of those born during this time has become dramatically secularized. A Deaf person should have the same opportunity as any hearing person to explore religious faith and understand the gospel in a language and cultural context that makes sense. They should not have this right taken away through neglect or direct resistance by those around them. They should have the right to accept, or reject, the most important question in the world... *"How do I make sense out of my existence; how do I reconnect with the God who created me?"*

If we remain stuck in a narrow definition of what is means to be part of Deaf culture, then what we are witnessing is the destruction of the culture. The first step is identifying the problem. The Deaf-World and ministries who serve Deaf people are in a crisis. The next step is to formulate a strategy for addressing the problem. On the other hand, if we recognize that being deaf in the 21st Century is radically different than at any previous time, adaptations are made and a scattered people can gather together in celebration and worship. We must remove the barriers to the Christian faith for all people. We need to accept the reality that Deaf people may be from different parts of the country, have different educational experiences, speak (or sign) with different accents, vote differently, think differently, behave differently and still share a common bond as members of the same dispersed community. If a person acquires information visually; he or she is a member of the Deaf community. We need to make sure they become a welcomed part of the mosaic of Deaf-World.

The exciting news is that God is unleashing a revival among the Deaf community unparalleled in history. He is doing this by calling his body of believers to let go of the past and embrace an exciting new future. The Apostle Paul writes, *"No, despite all these things, overwhelming victory is ours through Christ, who loved us. And I am convinced that nothing can ever separate us from his love. Death can't, and life can't. The angels can't, and the demons can't. Our fears for today, our worries about tomorrow, and even the powers of hell can't keep God's love away. Whether we are high above the sky or in the deepest ocean, nothing in all creation will ever be able to separate us from the love of God that is revealed in Christ Jesus our* Lord." (Romans 8:37-39, NLT).

꧁꧂

Personal Narrative ————————————————— Chad Entinger

My alarm clock is not my favorite possession. I love to sleep. Most mornings I consider my alarm clock a nuisance. Being Deaf, my alarm consists of a vibrator vibrating, lights flashing, and very loud beeping (yes, I can hear just a bit in my right ear). This chord of activity does its job—waking the heavy sleeper in me!

As the chord continues, I often hit my favorite button. You probably already know, per personal experience, which button it is. You've got it—the SNOOZE button. Ahh…how nice it is to hit the snooze button and get an extra nine minutes of sleep. It is only nice until I realize I've hit that snooze button a few too many times and I will be late for work, an appointment, or something else I planned! My, what fun it would be to witness someone else do all the scrambling, taking a shorter than usual shower, washing only your hair, applying less than usual strides of deodorant, putting on whatever clothes are closest to you in your closet, looking into your refrigerator and finding nothing convenient for breakfast, running out of your house, and driving ten miles an hour faster than usual! We may just discover how much of a fool we become ourselves when we are the ones doing all the scrambling to the rapid beats of our hearts.

I believe there is a Deaf alarm vibrating, flashing, and loudly beeping in an attempt to waken people, both Deaf and hearing, to the crisis facing the Deaf Community. Many Deaf people do *not* have Jesus as their Lord and Personal Savior. Estimates show there are at least 250 million Deaf people living in our world today.

Many of these Deaf people have yet to learn of the opportunity they can have of eternal life in Heaven (and the eternal consequences of sin). It has been reported that only 2% of Deaf people in the entire world are Christians.

Yes, we have a real crisis, or as Deaf Christians would sign it (with much emphasis!), "CRISIS REAL!" Too many Deaf people do not tie in Christian faith with the Deaf experience.

I believe the Evil One has been crafty at placing "snooze buttons" in Christians. We need to overcome the urge and tendency to hit our spiritual "snooze buttons" if we're going to, with God's help, raise the percentage of Deaf people who have a relationship with Jesus. Dare we become fools ourselves and keep on hitting the "snooze button?"

A Christian friend and I visited a man at his house. We were forewarned that he was not a Christian and had stopped attending church a long time ago. We began a casual conversation with him that ranged from learning about his family to his past schooling experiences to spiritual beliefs. Eventually, we asked him his thoughts about God.

"I am an atheist! I do not believe in God!" He responded.

I asked him, "Why do you NOT believe in God?"

He went on to answer, "My parents always forced me to go to church with them when I was growing up. But I never understood what was going on, because they had no interpreter and no one in the church knew sign language. They did not care about me or communicate with me."

"This doesn't seem like a very pleasant experience to me," were my thoughts.

He continued, "Speaking of church, I do not have any respect for preachers. I believe they are in the church to make money. I remember my preacher standing up in the front, on the stage, with a big smile while holding the offering plates after the offering had been collected."

My friend and I made repeated efforts to encourage the man to put aside his negative past experiences and understand that Jesus truly loves him, to no avail.

As we drove away we pondered how sad it was that this man felt he was "forced" to attend church while growing up. How sad it was that this church did not show the love of Jesus nor see this man through the eyes of Jesus. How sad that no one took the time to explain *clearly* Jesus Christ to him.

My best friend, Joe, was my roommate during college at Gallaudet University. When I was in graduate school, Joe worked for the Video Productions Department at Gallaudet. We lived in an apartment about 20 miles from the campus. Joe was prone to hitting that snooze button too many times. In fact, he was arriving to work late too often.

He realized he had a crisis. He realized he had to take action to correct this. He decided to set up his alarm clock (with the snooze button on it) on the other side of the bedroom. The next morning the lights would flash on and off. With the snooze button on the other side of the room, he had to get out of bed and walk across the room to turn off the alarm.

The Deaf alarm continues to go off. We continue to allow ourselves to hit the snooze button and allow this crisis to continue. Just how long can we continue to hit that snooze button? How long is too long?

My friends, for too many Deaf people, when Jesus comes again, it will have been too long. The time is now to wake up and act.

Discussion and Review

Deaf DIASPORA
Chapter 3—Crisis REAL

Expressions

Express how you would feel if you believed God could not understand your native language.

What are your observations about the general spiritual condition of our society-at-large and how do you think this has influenced the Deaf-World?

Challenge

The spiritual crisis is defined in terms of a crisis of culture, language, relationships and faith. Discuss the impact of each of these.

Why is the inability to "overhear" conversations within a hearing family a disadvantage for Deaf children in learning life skills? How were social skills communicated in earlier generations of the Deaf community?

What is the Deaf Alarm?

Scripture

"Anyone who comes and listens to me and obeys me is like someone who dug down deep and built a house on solid rock. When the flood came and the river rushed against the house, it was built so well that it didn't even shake. But anyone who hears what I say and doesn't obey me is like someone whose house wasn't built on solid rock. As soon as the river rushed against that house, it was smashed to pieces!" Luke 6:47-49

How does this Scripture apply to the crisis faced by the Deaf community? Why is careful planning and building on strong foundations so important, especially during a time of Diaspora?

Application

What are some of the things that may need to change in our traditional approach to ministry with the Deaf community?

Chapter 4—Next Generation

The sense of what it means to be Deaf is being
completely redefined for the 21ˢᵗ Century.

New Culture of Deafness

The good news is that Deaf culture is alive and well and experiencing a renewal largely through the Christian revival that is spreading across the nation. There is clearly still a "Deaf-World" and it is an exciting cultural experience. There are still people who are deeply connected with the Deaf-World through the efforts of their families. There are those with the good fortune of being born Deaf to Deaf parents and Deaf grandparents. This is an amazing blessing for an individual. There is a group of people God created in His image who are Deaf. They are not broken; they are individual reflections of the omnipotent God. The only one who defines our lives is the One who created us. *God has created us; only God defines us.* We can clearly state the Scriptural perspective on deafness as the cultural model. The Psalmist proclaims in Scripture, *"and I praise you because of the wonderful way you created me. Everything you do is marvelous! Of this I have no doubt."* (Psalm 139:14, CEV)

Our country has entered what has been termed as the "Postmodern" era of Christianity. Postmodernism (or modernity) was first identified in the 1930's but the term came into popular use during the 1970s.[62] It describes a basic shift in the worldview of this generation away from the absolutes of the past. Postmodernism affects the Deaf community but is not the fundamental issue threatening the existence of effective Deaf ministry. The characteristics of the new generation of Deaf youth are a macrocosm of the larger society. The single most important crisis confronting the Deaf community is the loss of a spiritual center due in large part to the onset of the Deaf Diaspora.

Survival of a culture involves adaptability. It is beneficial to become familiar with the body of works addressing the postmodern generation and effective strategies to reach young people with the gospel. The Amish are an example of a group who has attempted to hang on to the past to the exclusion of embracing the changes around them. Yet, even the Amish have adapted to some of the changes in the larger society. The Shakers did not adapt and no longer exist. Truth is eternal. Societies change. Cultures must adapt, or will be extinguished. Those involved with Deaf ministry must now bring an eternal gospel to a new generation.

Deaf ministry must adapt or it will perish. The truth of the gospel is eternal but we must be able to apply this truth to a new situation within a new culture. The first step is to understand the current situation more accurately and fully. The second step is to embrace a new model for Deaf ministry. God is greater than any challenges faced, including Diaspora. It is an exciting time to be called to Deaf ministry, although the Diaspora makes this ministry very difficult. Deaf ministry is a bigger issue than any one church, denomination, or para-church group can effectively address. It takes all of us working together for the glory of God. As the Body of Christ, we will adapt to these changes yet maintain the eternal truths that transcend all history. We will do our part to apply eternal truths in culturally relevant ways to a new generation of Deaf and hard of hearing individuals raised during the Deaf Diaspora.

The rest of this book addresses the way for this to grow, increase and develop a new generation of committed followers of Jesus Christ. These adolescents are building new skills for life as Christians who belong to the beautiful and proud lineage of the Deaf community. Make no mistake about it. They will look, act, and process information differently from earlier generations of Deaf. They live in a different world. They have different tastes and preferences. They use different technologies. But they are created Deaf and in the image of God. Our role is to help them discover this wonderful truth and experience personal faith.

There is a new experience of deafness that has emerged over the last twenty years of the 20th century. It is a blending of other cultures including the influences of the hearing world. This next generation of the Deaf community, those who are born in the 1980s and 1990s hold the promise of renewal and revival. The Christian faith, all but extinguished in the previous generation, is springing back to life in the lives of Deaf teenagers across the country. The focus of this book is on ministry with Deaf teenagers and young adults. The relational ministry principles can be applied to every age group but our priority is responding to the needs of the next generation. It is this generation of Deaf children and youth who will lead the Deaf community of the 21st century. What are the distinctive traits of this next generation of Deaf people? What is the *New Culture of Deafness*?

It is a culture of technology.

What seemed like science fiction a couple of decades ago is now common place. What seems like fantasy today may be reality in the near future. Deaf teenagers are influenced by the quality of software programs, speed of computers, video games, and creativity found on the Internet and through wireless connections. Their expectations are high. They want quality products. Production of brochures, banners, promotional materials, DVDs, websites and educational programs must meet their high expectations or else they will be ignored and discarded. It is not enough to tag the "Deaf" label on something; it must be done well or else these young people will move on to something more exciting, most likely in the secular market. Ministry must appeal to their needs as Deaf people familiar with technology and accustomed to excellence in marketing.

Technology is the gateway into a whole new world of opportunity and danger. The New Culture of Deafness is woven together (and sometimes driven apart) by technology. Information now moves about at cyber-speed. Hurtful rumors do as well. Internet messages are a part of this generation's daily conversations. I jokingly refer to the "Deaf Fatigue Syndrome" for those who work all day, chat all night on the Internet, and become physically exhausted. The ability to use the high-speed Internet for interpreting services opens up many work possibilities for the Deaf community.

As the concept of computer-generated, animated interpreters becomes a reality, the need for professional interpreters decreases. Video relay services and wireless Internet technology may allow Deaf people to carry their interpreters around in their pocket or purse. By the time you are reading this book, such a resource may be common in the marketplace. At this point, it is only at the early stages of development.[63]

One can imagine the new opportunities found in technology that more effectively connects the hearing and Deaf worlds. In the past, a small notepad and pencil were in the possession of virtually every Deaf adult. Now, young Deaf people use wireless technology to type messages to their friends or when ordering at the local fast food restaurant. The next generation of Deaf people will grow up with a strong sense of the importance and use of technology as part of the Deaf culture.

It is a culture of educational diversity.

One of the interesting dynamics of this next generation is the variety of educational experiences that an individual Deaf child has from pre-school to graduation from high school. In previous generations, people tended to stay in either the residential or the mainstreamed setting for most of their education. Now, with the mobility and educational options available in our society, we find many high school students who have received education in numerous settings over the years. Relatively few people remain exclusively in the residential setting. A much higher percentage of students remain mainstreamed for their entire schooling but many will spend at least some time at the residential school. This has the positive effective of mixing together the culture surrounding the Deaf schools and the diversity of the mainstreamed setting. The downside may be a constant adjustment required in the residential school setting for influences brought in by a revolving list of students. There are also a certain number of students who enter the residential school as high school students as a result of lack of success in the mainstreamed setting. They residential school must then deal with a number of problems and educational deficits with a short period of time for remediation.

There are very bright Deaf children and youth in both mainstreamed and residential settings. Attendance in one or the other may become significant in terms of who you know or went to school with but will not be a basis for inclusion or exclusion in identifying with the Deaf community. This diversity will evolve into a greater connection with one's favorite college or professional sports team than with the schools for the Deaf. There will not be the same widespread emotional connection with the residential schools of the Deaf in the next generation as with earlier generations.

The war over mainstreaming is drawing to a close but individual battles will continue. The reality is the new world of deafness will not include residential school identity as a significant part of the culture. Gallaudet and the National Technical Institute for the Deaf (NTID) will undoubtedly remain excellent institutions of higher learning and "keepers of the heritage" for the Deaf community but there will be a new generation of well-educated, successful Deaf adults who graduated from a variety of colleges. Because of advances in technology, people will have more choices to suit their educational needs and vocational goals. The New Culture of Deafness is one of educational diversity both individually and collectively.

It is a culture influenced by the media.

It still catches my eye when I see a Deaf teenager wearing a headset connected to a CD that is playing the newest teenage music hits. Like hearing teenagers, they like it loud, even louder! The next generation of Deaf people is living in a culture driven by the media. They are keenly aware of popular culture and influenced by advertising and marketing. They want to drink the same soft drink as other teenagers (usually bright red or yellow) and have opinions about the best cars, clothing, and video game players. This generation of Deaf is able to watch many first-run movies in theatres with open captioning (although not nearly often enough!) and can turn on the English subtitles on most DVDs. The media is driven by the market and the Deaf community spends money just like everyone else.

This generation is much more quickly in touch with current events and trends than earlier generations. One example is the two-way pager and other wireless technology. Regular news, sports, and weather updates are sent to these pagers. The Internet is full of advertisements and attractive video clips. Cable and satellite dish receivers bring hundreds of channels into the home. As people who process information visually, the media becomes a huge source of entertainment and information.

As this generation becomes adults, they are facing the same pressures, influences, and opportunities from the media (positive and negative) as anyone else living in the United States. It becomes much more difficult for the older Deaf community to attract young people to activities at the Deaf club or other traditional venues. What it means to the church, is our programming must now appeal to an audience accustomed to high levels of technology and creative marketing. We need to be able to produce excellence in programming and presentation.

It is a culture of communication tolerance.

There will come a day when the comment that someone "thinks hearing" will be passé. English will become more visual (because of technology and the media) and sign language will become more influenced by its contact with spoken, written and signed English. There are various regional and initialized signs for McDonald's restaurants. No one really cares what the correct ASL sign is, everyone just wants to stop and eat! The lack of concern is not a statement against the legitimacy and proper place of ASL as the natural language of the Deaf. The higher value is on successful communication and connection between friends and acquaintances. Many of those who interact with the next generation of Deaf are hearing people or other Deaf people who grew up in mainstreamed environments. This translates into tolerance of "whatever works" in getting an idea across—signing, speech, gestures, written notes, emails, instant messages, and so forth. Relationships in this generation and successful communication are the higher priority than loyalty to a particular language preference.

Historically, the lines of separation were more distinct. The Deaf community kept ASL to themselves and would "code-shift" when hearing people were around. Those who were speech-readers and used verbal skills would never sign and generally looked down upon those who used any form of sign language. There is an increased openness of young Deaf people to use whatever works to engage in meaningful communication. The code-shifting is in relation to the setting; not whether someone is hearing or Deaf. The lines are more blurred now although the primary goal is still clear; Deaf people want (and deserve) full access to and exchange of information.

In the hearing world, some people speak with a strong accent. Almost every hearing person who signs does so with a "hearing" accent. The most skilled signers and interpreters are complimented with a *"Wow. She (or he) signs like Deaf."* The hearing accent is virtually gone. One can look past the odd sounding words (or in our case, the odd choice or form of signs) to connect with the person behind the words or signs. There is no need to feel guilty about signing with an accent; just continue to improve your communication skills as a way of life. The focus of this generation is relationships.

Let me hasten to say, this is nothing new in the Deaf world. The Deaf community has long been a model of tolerance for efforts to understand, and be understood, by others. This is an amazing cultural trait that deserves recognition and respect. The hearing world has not been nearly so tolerant. Those who would ostracize other Deaf people for never learning ASL fluently will cease to dominate the culture of the past two decades. The New Culture of Deafness will return to an earlier day of inclusion of the differences. The sign for "equal" and "fair" are almost synonymous and it is an appropriate description of the coming culture. It is only fair for anyone's preferred style of communication to be considered equal with all others. The primary goal is "to know and be known" through meaningful relationships.

It is a culture of the Diaspora.

The Deaf Diaspora holds tremendous danger for the Deaf community. At the same time, it will become a part of the culture and history of the Deaf community. How the Deaf-World survives the Diaspora depends on a willingness to accept this reality and adapt to the changes. It becomes a culture of the Diaspora.

Slavery is a painful part of the history of our world. For the African people, slavery was particularly destructive because of the brutal nature of the "chattel" form of slavery when Africans were forced into the Americas. Other cultures throughout history practiced slavery that was not so cruel (i.e. Hagar with Abraham, Joseph in Egypt or the Jews in Babylon) although still morally wrong. The African bondage in the Americas was particularly unjust. However, the African community survived and evolved into the African-American community with a rich heritage and history. Their history did not begin in bondage; they are descendents of kingdoms and cultures in other lands. They could have let this Diaspora become the end of their culture. Instead, they kept the stories of the homeland alive but adapted to the new culture by pulling together as a people.

The Diaspora becomes a bond between diverse Deaf people who similarly experience dispersion.

The Diaspora is now a part of the Deaf experience just as it is for the Jewish people, Native Americans, African-Americans and hundreds of other cultures before us. It is now a culture that is defined, in part, by the Diaspora itself. Every coming together of the scattered Deaf community is a homecoming. Every introduction to another person from the scattered population of Deaf and hard of hearing is a reason for joy. Every building of a friendship with a person who has struggled alone for years and years is a cause for celebration. God has created us to be in community with one another. He wants his children to show his love to each other and the world. The worst prison in the world is isolation. The greatest experience of all is being welcomed home—as part of the New Culture of Deafness.

Deaf festivals that celebrate Deaf culture and arts still exist and the largest gathering to celebrate the Deaf-World was held in 2002, "Deaf Way II" hosted by Gallaudet University. Deaf Way II was an incredible expression of the importance of Deaf culture and heritage. Almost 10,000 participants and over 400 Deaf performing, visual, and literary artists came from around the world for this event.[64] The goals of Deaf Way II describe important elements of the Deaf-World:

- Encourage cross-cultural and cross-continent exchanges through an international conference on language, culture, history, and art of Deaf and hard of hearing people.

- Examine technology use by, for, and on deaf people, and consider the interconnectedness of deaf, hard of hearing, and hearing people in an increasingly technologically sophisticated world.

- Celebrate the visual, performing, and literary arts of Deaf and hard of hearing people through a Cultural Arts Festival.

- Foster greater tolerance and understanding among deaf, hard of hearing and hearing people through scholarly discussions and experiential cultural events for participants, and extensive outreach to the general public.

- Heighten opportunities for Deaf and hard of hearing people by bringing to light our artistic, leadership and professional capabilities and diverse contributions to societies around the world.[65]

Every Diaspora needs a homecoming. The first Deaf Way was in 1989 at the zenith of Deaf pride and awareness. The second one (described above) was thirteen years later. Note the ages of the Deaf Baby Boomers in 2002; many of these who were college students would be in their mid- to late-thirties and at a point in their lives when they may have the time, energy, money and interest in gathering. Obviously, all 10,000 participants were not in this age bracket but it is an interesting factor to consider.

Four Examples of the Next Generation *Where are the Deaf examples?!*

Marlee Matlin was clearly identified with Deaf-World during the height of the Deaf Baby Boom generation and continues as a respected and successful actress. Marlee broke onto the national scene as Sarah Norman in the movie "Children of a Lesser God" in 1986 for which she received an Academy Award for Best Actress. She was only 21 years old and became the youngest recipient of the Best Actress Oscar.[66] Matlin continued as a popular actress in a number of television series and movies. Matlin is an example of someone strongly part of the Deaf-World who exerted her rights as an individual to use whatever means possible to understand and be understood. As an adult, Matlin took speech therapy to improve her opportunities for acting parts. She decided to speak for her acceptance speech instead of signing. She also uses ASL as her primary mode of communication. Matlin reflects the power of Deaf identity and the willingness to operate in the language of the majority culture when necessary. In an interview she says, *"When I learned to sign and speak at the same time, the whole world opened up to me. That's the beauty of encouraging kids who are deaf to use whatever it takes to communicate."*[67] Matlin exemplifies the strength of Deaf identity and is a role model for the front edge of the next generation.

Heather Whitestone McCallum danced her way into our awareness as the winner of the 1995 Miss America contest. She was awesome as she explained her S.T.A.R.S. (Success Through Action and Realization of your dreamS) program for personal excellence during the interview part of the contest. The STARS program has five points representing *"a positive attitude, a goal, a willingness to work hard, a realistic look at your problems and a support team."*[68] Heather's charisma, intelligence, beauty, and charm placed her clearly at the head of the group and she was chosen as the new Miss America. She later wrote her autobiography, *"Listening With My Heart"* (1996, Doubleday). Heather was criticized by some in the Deaf community for using her voice, signing in exact English, and not really being part of the Deaf culture. Heather decided to have surgery for a Cochlear Implant to improve her hearing. Most recently, she has become a spokesperson to promote the development of speech reading/verbal skills. She has little visible connection with the signing Deaf-World although she may be a competent signer. Although many view this as a long-standing disagreement between proponents of oral communication versus signing, in many ways, Heather was a forerunner of the New Culture of Deafness and was caught in the crush of the transition between eras. Instead of attacking her, a more productive approach would be to encourage her to build her ASL skills and recognize her right to choose her own path as a Deaf person.

Deanne Bray-Kotur, the actress who stars on the PAX television show, *Sue Thomas, F.B. Eye* was born in 1971 and Deaf since birth. She was raised with both speech and sign language. She is a fully participating part of Deaf-World. She was part of the Non-Traditional Casting Project, Deaf West Theatre and the Greater Los Angeles Council on Deafness. She hosted a Deaf program, *Caption This.* In addition, she has been a math and science teacher for Deaf high school students and was working on her Master's degree in Education. She originated a literacy program called *The Little Bookworm Club.* Bray-Kotur signs excellent ASL and verbalizes English beautifully. Deanne Bray-Kotur's ability to connect with the hearing world while maintaining a seeming comfortable sense of herself as a Deaf person is impressive and notable. Although Bray-Kotur herself is an excellent role model although the television show may inadvertently create unreal expectations as to the speech reading and verbal skills of other Deaf people, particularly children.

The clearest and most current example of the New Culture of Deafness is seen in Christy Smith from the reality show *Survivor—The Amazon* fame. Others will certainly follow as even greater examples but she is a visible prototype of the next generation. Smith was raised in the outdoor environment of Aspen, Colorado, where she developed a love for nature and adventure. She is an athletic young woman whose motto is *Challenge Yourself.* Like many Deaf of her generation, she began speech therapy at an early age and along with a minimal hearing ability became proficient at speech-reading and speaking. Christy first interacted with other Deaf children at the Aspen Camp School for the Deaf but grew in stronger connection with the Deaf-World when she transferred as a junior to the Model Secondary School for the Deaf in Washington, D.C. located on the campus of Gallaudet University. She graduated from college at Gallaudet with a Bachelor's degree in Sociology and Criminology in 2000. She worked in a juvenile detention center and with abused women. After graduation, she lived for five months in Costa Rica, working with the Deaf community.[69]

Christy Smith's experience on *Survivor* was a classic example of this next generation; she is a competitor. She chose to be on *Survivor* to promote Deaf awareness. Smith used her wits, charm, intelligence, persuasion and physical skills to stay in the game. She would use whatever means available to her to communicate with the other contestants. It was her choice not to use an interpreter in the contest (which drew some criticism). Smith has a clear sense of Deaf identity but her values, skills, strengths and weaknesses are not unlike anyone else in the game. Deaf people of this generation do not have a passion for protecting "pure" Deaf culture; they want to compete. They want to win. Participation is not enough; they want to *"Outwit, Outplay, Outlast."*[70] Smith describes her personal mission to, "provide Deaf Awareness, bridge the gap between deaf and hearing, and teaching sign language to youth."[71] Smith fully embraces her connection with Deaf-World and signs proficiently. She is also able to communicate by any means necessary. Since the completion of the show, she is now host of a children's show, *Challenge Yourself* to promote Deaf awareness while learning about the "great outdoors."[72]

The point of highlighting these four individuals (who are in the public eye) is to show the range of Deaf experience that all qualify as part of Deaf culture. Use of verbal skills is *not* the indication of the New Culture of Deafness, *diversity* is. Many of the next generation would choose never to use voice or speech-reading. This choice is their God-given right and is the anchor upon which the Deaf culture truly depends. From strong ASL to signed English to speech-reading/verbal skills—it does not really matter—all who comprehend through vision (or touch in the case of Deaf-Blind) are welcome here in the next generation.

Literacy is vital for personal success and safety in our culture. Regardless of one's native language, English is the primary language of commerce, education, and communication in America. Rejection of speech should never be an excuse for rejection of literacy skills. Educational access is an opportunity for all people to become literate, and for many, scholarly. To remain a strong and free nation, we must maximize the resources and contributions of all our citizens. This requires a commitment to improve the written comprehension and expressive skills of all those being educated including Deaf children. This is a foundational value upon which all educators, parents, and leaders in the Deaf community agree: literacy is *vital*.

A 21st Century Youth Program

Let me introduce you to some fictional Deaf teenagers. These characters are based on a compilation of the background of various young Deaf people known to the author. Any similarity to specific individuals is purely coincidental. The names have been chosen randomly based on the first seven letters of the alphabet. This group is an accurate portrayal of the incredible diversity of this generation of Deaf youth. Also note that having seven Deaf young people in one ministry is a significant number. I suggest that people unfamiliar with ministry to Deaf teenagers use a mathematical factor of "times ten"—meaning the effort to attract and involve Deaf teenagers is somewhat equivalent to connecting with ten times that many hearing teens. This size Deaf teen ministry would be similar to having seventy secondary school students in a hearing youth group program. That would be a fairly impressive number in most churches or ministries.

Effective Deaf ministry must recognize and adapt to the needs of this new generation. These young people reflect the diversity of the New Culture of Deafness.

Aleah	white female; attended residential school for the Deaf until high school but now is fully mainstreamed; junior
Bryan	African-American male; has attended residential school for the Deaf for his entire education; senior
Christina	Mexican-American female; mainstreamed for elementary school but transferred to residential school; 8th grader
Deon	white male; mainstreamed all his life; a dozen other Deaf students at his school; unsuccessful Cochlear Implant; has cerebral palsy; in 9th grade
Erica	Asian female (adopted at age 4); self-contained classroom with other Deaf students; currently in 7th grade for second year
Federico	Latino male; attended residential school for Deaf-Oral program for most of life but now mainstreamed in local school system; senior
Gracie	African-American female; in Deaf-Oral program; mainstreamed for part of the day; has Cochlear Implant; Tenth grader

Notice the diversity of communication preferences. Aleah is proficient in pure ASL and never uses her voice to communicate. Gracie never signs and depends exclusively on speech-reading and voice. Deon falls right in the middle and code shifts depending on with whom he is communicating. The following chart shows the continuum of communication preferences among this youth group. The two variables reflected here are ASL and English-signing ratios and uses of signing versus speech. Remember, this is not data from a scientific study; it is a chart for describing a concept.

Now, let's take a look at the other demographic information. We have four females and three males. Our group has a range of ages from Erica, a girl in seventh grade (who was adopted from China) in a self-contained classroom within a mainstreamed setting to Bryan, an African-American senior ready to graduate from a residential school for the Deaf. Christina's parents speak little or no English and rely on a sibling who is essentially trilingual at a conversational skill level. The other Latino in the group, Federico, comes from a well-educated Venezuelan family. His family maintains strong emotional ties with their native country but only speak English at home with their Deaf son. Deon has cerebral palsy that affects his balance and academic performance. Aleah is regularly on the honor roll and is a star athlete on the school's basketball team.

New Culture of Deafness Communication Continuum

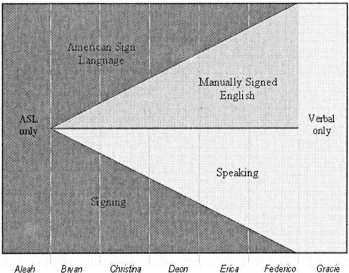

	Aleah	Bryan	Christina	Deon	Erica	Federico	Gracie
ASL	100%	90%	60%	50%	40%	10%	0
MSE	0	10%	40%	50%	60%	90%	100%
Signing	100%	90%	80%	50%	20%	10%	0
Speaking	0	10%	20%	50%	80%	90%	100%

What do they share in common? They are all Deaf. They all depend on their eyes to gather information and process information through the visual centers of their brains. They want to be together and with other Deaf teenagers. They are bright, fun, creative, passionate, emotional, and confronting the challenges of the teen years as Deaf people. They all find visual jokes funny and are puzzled at much of "hearing" humor. They all are willing to accept each other without judgment and want to have fun. They thrive on the attention and love of Christian adults who provide positive activities and young Christian Deaf role models. They all have questions and concerns about life and share a common experience of being left out of many of the venues that provide those answers. They take care of each other and encourage each other. Sometimes they fuss and occasionally fight. They recognize in each other a common struggle to know and be known;

to enjoy friendship. They want to have hearing and Deaf friends and make their own choices. They want to understand their roles in their families. They share a passion for understanding the mystery of God's incredible love for them. They are part of a community of people who experience life similarly. They are Deaf. They are a microcosm of the next generation of Deaf people. They comprise the characteristics of the New Culture of Deafness. They are individuals who share life together.

Deaf ministry with teenagers is tough, arguably one of the most challenging ministries possible. If you are a hearing adult, you are crossing at least two cultural divides, Deaf and youth, before you even confront any socio-economic differences. Simply finding Deaf teenagers is difficult; the schools cannot release this type of information. Dealing with the lack of understanding about youth ministry within the Deaf-World and the equal ignorance about the Deaf experience in the youth world is exhausting. Deaf teenagers generally have a huge accumulation of emotions, frustrations, and hurt from years of feeling left out of the hearing world. Many of these teens struggle with fundamental issues of trust. It is difficult to find young Christian Deaf adults (the missing generation) who are willing and able to invest their lives into the lives of these young people. As in many helping ministries, Deaf ministry may attract insecure hearing people who have an unhealthy emotional need to be needed. For these reasons and more, Deaf ministry with teenagers has been almost non-existent over the past twenty years. There seems to be an unusually high burnout rate among leaders who work with Deaf teenagers.

But remember how precious in God's sight are Aleah, Bryan, Christina, Deon, Erica, Federico, Gracie and all the other Deaf teenagers in your community. God is passionate for them. God is calling a whole new generation of sharp, talented young Deaf, hard of hearing and hearing people to this mission. This 21st Century Deaf youth program needs large numbers of Christian adults who love Jesus, love each other and love Deaf teenagers. Are you one of these adults? Has God touched your heart and given you a passion for this ministry? Again, let me warn you. It is a difficult, time consuming investment of your life for a very small number of people. Will you leave the ninety-nine for the one? Are you willing to find new, creative ways to reach this next generation of Deaf teenagers applying the wisdom of proven youth ministry methodology? Will you help recapture the spiritual center of the New Culture of Deafness?

Personal Narrative ————————————————————Chad Entinger

At the time of writing, I am a few years away from having lived three decades. I consider my own life to be a good reflection of the radical changes that have occurred across the Deaf Community over the last thirty years.

In 1977, I lost my hearing at age two due to Spinal Meningitis. Upon finding out that I had lost my hearing, my parents welcomed advice from professionals, who encouraged my parents to learn Signing Exact English (SEE). Also, per advice, they raised me with an emphasis on being oral.

The 1970s were a decade marked by hearing professionals encouraging Deaf children to be mainstreamed instead of being schooled in a Residential program. Today, there continues to be a decline in the percentage of Deaf children schooled in Residential programs. Prior to the early 1970s, approximately eighty percent of Deaf children were in residential programs and twenty percent were in mainstream programs. Today, three decades later, the numbers are inverted. Approximately eighty percent of Deaf children are schooled in mainstream programs, whereas, twenty percent of Deaf children are in residential programs.

I spent a large portion of the 1980s in a mainstream program with an interpreter. I also spent a large portion of this time enduring the lack of awareness and understanding of Deaf people among teachers and classmates. During this decade, I received my very first TTY (teletype phone).

Prior to 1988, there did not seem to be much awareness among hearing people regarding Deaf people, their abilities, and American Sign Language.

One powerful movement in the spring of 1988 seemed to change this—the famous and world known "Deaf President Now" protest conducted by the students of Gallaudet University. The students demanded, after the Board of Trustees selected a hearing woman who did not know sign language as the president of the college, that the Board of Trustees instead select a qualified Deaf person to be the president. This was a successful movement as the hearing woman resigned and the Board selected Dr. I. King Jordan as the very first Deaf president of Gallaudet University. TTY's were used when Phil Bravin, the chairman of the Board of Trustees, called Greg Hlibok, student leader of the protest, to inform him about the Board's selection of the first Deaf president. This protest, with the aid of worldwide publicity, helped many people become aware of Deaf people, their culture, and their language.

A big change in my life occurred shortly after this protest. In 1989, I transferred from a mainstream program and enrolled in a residential school—the

Minnesota State Academy for the Deaf. I spent my high school years there learning American Sign Language which is quite different from Signing Exact English and Oralism.

After the protest and during the 1990s there was a rapid influence of people learning sign language. Many more schools and college programs started offering sign language classes. It seemed to become more commonplace for Deaf people to enter restaurants and have a waiter or waitress know some, if not a lot, of sign language.

Sometimes, this is not always the case and misconceptions arise. I had a Deaf friend who once went into a fast food restaurant. As he walked up to the cashier, he gestured, "CAN'T HEAR." The cashier pointed with her index finger to indicate, "Just wait a minute." The cashier walked behind the cooking area. My friend waited for her to come back. And she came back...with a Braille menu!

I spent a major portion of the 1990s at Gallaudet University. I became quite independent, relying on televisions with built-in chips for closed captioning, e-mail, Internet, and pagers.

The 1990s and early 2000s has been an era that has witnessed a boom in technology. Closed captioned television, E-mail, Internet, and pagers become favorites of Deaf people.

From Signing Exact English and Oralism to American Sign Language...from depending on my parents to tell me what was happening on television to the independence of Closed Captioning on television...from being mainstreamed in a public school to being schooled in residential school...from snail mail to e-mail...from TTYs to TDDs to Sidekick pagers and Video Relay Service...from depending on others to call to get information for me to getting information myself on the Internet...from lack of awareness to being aware...

Indeed, there have been radical changes in the Deaf experience in my own life over the past three decades.

And yes, over the last three decades of the 20th Century, there has been a radical change in the Deaf experience in the United States.

It seems Deaf people are becoming more and more independent. At the same time, it seems they are becoming less and less dependent on God.

The Bill of Rights for the
NEW CULTURE OF DEAFNESS

I. I have the right as a Deaf or Hard of hearing individual to have my own unique traits, opinions, experiences and perspectives.

II. I have the right to be accepted as part of the Deaf community regardless of the mode(s) of communication I use.

III. I have the right to call myself "Deaf;" I am a proud heir of my Deaf cultural legacy.

IV. I have the right to proclaim my deafness not as a disability but as how I was created by God.

V. I have the right not to be referred to as "d/Deaf;" it is an artificial means of excluding people.

VI. I have the right to enjoy music and dance as part of my desire for self-expression and personal enjoyment.

VII. I have the right to attend school in a mainstreamed setting and still maintain a Deaf identity and connection.

VIII. I have the right to attend school in a residential setting and still enjoy my friendships with those in the "hearing" world.

IX. I have the right to use technology to communicate, including any that improves what hearing I may have.

X. I have the right to develop a personal faith in God in a way that makes sense to me as a Deaf person.

I am part of the NEW CULTURE OF DEAFNESS.

Discussion and Review

Deaf DIASPORA
Chapter 4—Next Generation

Expressions

Describe the technology you use on a daily basis. How has your life been affected by technology? What are the positive and negative aspects of the influence of technology?

Describe your educational experience while growing up. What were your schools like? What do you hold in common with other people in your age group and what is different about your experience?

Challenge

Describe how the isolation from others in the Deaf community has been detrimental to this generation of Deaf.

Our entire society has been in moral decline over the past forty years. Why may this be even more pronounced in this most recent generation of Deaf?

Describe how technology, education, and the media influence the Deaf community in the 21st century.

Explain how the Diaspora has become part of the New Culture of Deafness.

Scripture

"I will rescue them from all the places where they were scattered on a day of clouds and darkness. I will bring them out from the nations and gather them from the countries, and I will bring them into their own land. I will pasture them on the mountains of Israel, in the ravines and in all the settlements in the land." Ezekiel 34:12-13

Pray for God to help you partner with Him to *"rescue them from all the places where they were scattered"* and find ways to minister to the dispersed community.

Application

Consider some ways to use technology to minister within the Deaf community. What are some practical ideas that may be applied? What are the dangers of using too much technology in ministry?

Waves THREE
Section II

"If only you had paid attention to my commandments!
Then your well-being would have been like a river, and your righteousness
like the waves of the sea." (Isaiah 48:18, NASB)

Those familiar with the ocean know that waves come in sets of three; usually the third wave is the largest, and for surfers, the best! I grew up in Florida and remember the excitement of sitting on a surfboard and recognizing a coming set of waves. The first wave comes in; it is noticeably larger than the choppy waves that preceded it. Immediately behind it, an even larger second wave brings smiles to the faces of surfers as they sit on their surfboards in anticipation. Some turn and ride the second wave but many continue looking beyond. When the third wave of the set begins to rise out of the ocean, tan bodies rotate onto their stomachs and begin paddling furiously towards the shore. Everyone is trying to "catch the wave." If you do not have enough momentum and speed then the wave will pass underneath you and you slide back into the trough behind the wave. If your timing and skill are on target, you can feel the rise of the water beneath you and sense of movement and increasing speed. You paddle hard and in a flash, spring to your feet. You are now riding the third wave of the set. A whole row of surfers glides gracefully back and forth across the face of the wave on their way towards the shore.

This metaphor holds true for societal patterns. Movements often occur in waves depending on the variables at the time of the movement. These waves are predictable though sometimes discernable only in retrospect. Waves also tend to come in patterns that may be repeated through history. In a previous chapter, I described the "Lost Generation" of World War I. A similar experience happened to the generation of soldiers who were in the Vietnam Conflict during the late 1960s and early 1970s. There is a moral vacuum that tends to follow war. Patterns tend to repeat themselves.

There is a necessity for using generalizations when making observations of societal movements yet there are always exceptions to generalizations. We can describe the "Missing Generation" of the Christian Deaf community while recognizing there are some notable exceptions to this generalization. A few inspiring Christian ministers emerge during these mostly lean years. In fact, sometimes when society is the most confusing, God's presence is the clearest. When a Deaf person became a Christian during the closing decades of the 20th Century, he or she would often become strong in faith because of the general resistance experienced from others in the secular Deaf community.

The Waves THREE are divided by two decades each: 1960s and 1970s, 1980s and 1990s, and 2000s and 2010s. I would like to think of the Third Wave as *the wave of the future* but in reality, we will likely enter another new era during the 2020s. No one knows what the future will bring. There may be a modification of the Third Wave or the beginning of a new set of Waves. It may be the Fourth Wave. There may be the lull between sets of waves. Only God knows. But for now, let's evaluate this set of three waves of Deaf ministry.

In this section about Waves THREE, there will be individual ministries that do not fit the generalizations being made. There will be ministries in one wave that operate like ministries in the next wave; they were ahead of their time. There will be other ministries (the ones that survive) that evolve from one wave to the next wave to the next. Look at the general trends and characteristics being described while accepting a reasonable level of individual exceptions. The value in making generalizations is that they allow us to analyze, learn and adapt. Do not assume that every ministry during each wave has all the traits of that particular wave. They may have one or two characteristics that fit in a different category. Also recognize that these types of generalizations may be statistically quantifiable but in this book are only observations. If I were able to present enough concrete data to convince you of these observations, this book would be much more technical, extensive, lengthy and difficult to understand. These observations are based largely on anecdotal information even, though supported by cursory research.

The First and Second Waves of Deaf Ministry were vital during those eras for reaching the Deaf-World for Christ. The First Wave ministries trained many of the Second Wave leaders. The Second Wave ministries have held on to the Christian faith in the midst of the Crisis REAL that was described earlier in the book. Many of the Third Wave leaders grew up in the Second Wave. They are the ones who helped keep the Christian faith alive during the early years of the Diaspora.

We must draw on the strengths of the First and Second Waves of Deaf ministry to reach our world for Christ during the Third Wave. We must remain committed to the fundamental principles of the First Wave that passionately wanted to share the gospel with the next generation and recognized the primary role of Scripture. Likewise, we must cling to the principles of the Second Wave, including the importance of Deaf culture, identity, ASL, and the importance of Deaf-led ministries with Christian Deaf role models. The reality of the Third Wave is that this new generation of Deaf is distinct and lives in a new world. We must adapt to find new ways of reaching the Deaf community with the eternal gospel of Jesus Christ. We can learn from the past without being trapped in it.

There are always many variables that cannot be anticipated when predicting societal patterns. No one could have anticipated the impact on our country (and world) of that one fateful morning in September of 2001 when terrorists attacked. A dramatic event can totally change cultural predictions. The societal patterns that helped us chart a course before the attack were disrupted and redefined in light of the trauma. The same is true when predicting religious patterns. Change can sometimes be rapid and unpredictable but one thing is certain, there is always going to be change. It is important to develop skills for adaptation without losing focus on fundamental principles. This is part of what gives us security as we enter the unknown.

The Bible is full of examples of major changes that impacted the lives of God's people. No one knows the future. Kingdoms rise and fall in ways that remind us of a changing shoreline; sand castles may even be washed away by a single wave. Given enough time, even a rocky coast gives way for new formations. The only thing that is dependable in this world is God's Spirit and His Word. God guides us as we face the rising and falling of the tides of change. We press forward and embrace the future with confidence, vision, and understanding. A new day presents a new set of challenges. It makes sense to seek God's wisdom when we are responding to life's variables. God will lead us through.

General Characteristics of the Waves THREE of Deaf Ministry

First WAVE Deaf ministry   *1960s and 1970s*
    Traits of the First Wave
        Individual leadership
        Hearing-led
        Church-based
        Evangelical
        Bible-centered teaching
        Preaching and signed music
        Inclusion with hearing (interpreting)
        "All God's Children" (Deaf are not different)
        Manually Signed English
        Priority on English comprehension

Second WAVE Deaf ministry   *1980s and 1990s*
    Traits of the Second Wave
        Team leadership
        Deaf-led
        Revival and traveling ministries
        Instructional
        Cultural awareness and fellowship
        Focus on drama
        Indigenous Deaf churches
        Deaf identity and rights (We are unique)
        American Sign Language
        Priority on teaching ASL skills and Deaf Culture

Third WAVE Deaf ministry   *2000s and 2010s*
    Traits of the Third Wave
        Individual and team leadership
        Gifts—diversity and unity
        Large geographical regions
        Missions
        Outreach and relational ministry
        Technology, drama, Deaf-music, basic Gospel
        Inclusive and unique programming
        Equal access to the Gospel
        ASL with acceptance of other communications styles
        Priority on personal connection

General Characteristics of the
Waves THREE of Deaf Ministry

First Wave	Second Wave	Third Wave
Individual Leadership	Team Leadership	Individual and Team Leadership
Hearing-led	Deaf-led	Gifts–Diversity and Unity
Church-based	Revival and Traveling Ministries	Large Geographic Regions
Evangelical	Instructional	Missions
Bible-centered Teaching	Cultural Awareness and Fellowship	Outreach and Relational Ministry
Preaching and Signed Hymns	Focus on Drama	Technology, DraMuSign, Deaf-Music, Basic Gospel
Inclusion with Hearing	Indigenous Deaf Churches	Inclusive and unique programming
"All God's Children" (Deaf are not different)	Deaf Identity and Rights (We are unique)	Equal Access to the Gospel
Manually Signed English	American Sign Language	ASL with acceptance of other communication styles
Priority on English Comprehension	Priority on Teaching ASL skills and Deaf Culture	Priority on Personal Relationships
1960s–1970s	*1980s–1990s*	*2000s–2010s*

"Deaf Diaspora: The Third Wave of Deaf Ministry" by Bob Ayres was published by iUniverse in 2004.

Chapter 5—First Wave

*The First Wave of evangelical Deaf ministry was during the
1960s and 1970s, when life was very different from today.*

This is not the first wave of Deaf ministry in the history of the church; it is the
first wave of this "set of waves." There were incredible examples of ministry during the late 1800s and early 1900s. The First Wave of this set was part of the general revival of the 1950s influencing the Deaf-World during the 1960s. The
impact of evangelists like Billy Graham created an excitement about the potential of our country to turn our hearts toward God. The evangelical protestant
church was growing rapidly throughout the latter part of the 1950s. The
Southern Baptist church in particular was spreading rapidly and establishing mission churches throughout the country.

In contrast, the 1960s brought a sense of mankind's ability to address our own
problems. President John F. Kennedy announced we could put a man on the
moon by the end of the decade and we believed him. Corporations were growing
and American productivity was the envy of the world. It was a time of scientific
and medical discovery, the Atom bomb and the Communist threat. There was a
growing emphasis on social and political solutions to society's problems.

At the same time, there was a storm brewing. The crisis of the war in Vietnam,
widespread racism, cruel segregation of the races, the changing role of women in
society, the explosion of recreational drug use and the "sexual revolution" were all
to slam our country during the same ten year period from the middle of the
1960s into the middle of the 1970s. The enormous numbers of post-World War
II births created a generation knows as the "Baby Boomers" who exacerbated this
already unstable environment. Our country became driven by a youth culture
due to sheer numbers of young people. The tension between generations was
intense and young people had a widespread distrust of the *Establishment* which
was a code-word for those in positions of power. We were a divided nation on
many fronts, and hostility would occasionally flare up in the form of protests, sit-
ins, and even riots.

Now, where were the Deaf during this period of time? Where were they being educated? How did they receive information? Where were they gathered? How were they relating to their families and society in general?

Remember, access to information was dramatically different for the Deaf community from what it is today. There were no VCRs or videotapes. There was no Internet, or IMs (instant messages), or two-way pagers. The only telephone access was through the old TTY machine that was a huge, teletypewriter that stood about four-feet tall, required reams of paper and a lot of space. There was no telephone Relay service. There were few skilled interpreters other than some of the CODAs (Children of Deaf Adults) and a few educators and religious leaders. There were few of the legal protections afforded Deaf individuals that are in place today during this pre-ADA era. During this pre-ADA era, there were only three major television networks and no closed captioning. Other than the newspaper, most information about current events came to Deaf people through hearing people. This put interpreters and hearing ministers in a significant position of power and influence over the lives of many Deaf individuals.

There existed a natural buffer between the turmoil of the hearing world and the islands of Deaf culture and relationships found in the Deaf-World that would later be stripped away. Eventually, the changes brought about by the 1960s and 1970s would also shape Deaf-World. There was urgency in preparing young Deaf people to face the radical changes happening in the hearing world that would eventually affect the Deaf-World. The evangelical community recognized the huge need and opportunity for ministry to the Deaf community and this created the First Wave of Deaf ministry.

Most of the residential schools for the Deaf kept students for the majority of the school year and sent them home only during holidays and summer. Because students were staying over the weekends, many schools required attendance at church activities. Religious instruction and worship was a normal part of life in the Deaf-World. Most of the schools for the Deaf had chaplains from a variety of denominations who lead in numerous religious activities including administering sacraments, worship, catechism and Biblical instruction. Most of this ministry was centered on the residential schools and tended to be denominational and sectarian in nature. This was a time of an open door to the gospel for many Deaf people. This environment of tolerance for religion by the state allowed for a wave of Deaf ministry across the nation. This was the background for the First Wave of Deaf ministry.

Defining traits of the First Wave
1st Wave
1960s and 1970s

Individual leadership
Hearing-led
Church-based
Evangelical
Bible-centered teaching
Preaching and signed hymns
Inclusion with Hearing (interpreting)
"All God's Children" (Deaf are not different)
Manually Signed English
Priority on English comprehension

Individual leadership—One of the characteristics of First Wave ministries was a single individual who provided religious instruction and program leadership. This was often a minister or missionary with a theological background who sensed a calling to ministry with the Deaf. These leaders may have developed a support team of Deaf members and worked on training indigenous leaders for the ministry but decisions reflected the top-down approach to management, as was a common style of leadership during the 1960s and 1970s. In some cases, it was an interpreter in charge of the Deaf ministry. At times, this person may have assumed an authoritative role with the ministry. It would be all too easy to become enmeshed in the needs of the Deaf people, and behave in a patronizing fashion, intentionally or not. Decisions were often handed from the top down and Deaf people were expected to cooperate with decisions made.

Within this organizational paradigm and during this era, there may have emerged a tendency for the Deaf leadership to be chosen based largely on their ability to operate effectively in a hearing world. In some situations those who possessed strong English skills were chosen in positions of leadership over more qualified individuals with a stronger ASL background and communication style.[73] There are notable exceptions to this dynamic on a national level but this problem was more evident within local churches. This is one of the inherent dangers when one cultural group is choosing the leadership for another cultural group. As outsiders it is difficult to discern who is truly most qualified to lead within the other cultural group. This system of top-down, individual leadership in ministries put the power into the hands of a single person and usually, a hearing interpreter or minister.

Hearing-led—The 1960s and 1970s were an era of strong evangelistic efforts to reach the world for Christ. For example, the Southern Baptist Convention launched a plan in 1976 called *Bold Mission Thrust* to reach the entire world with the gospel by the end of the 20th Century. This missionary mindset came from the hearing world to the Deaf world as one might bring the message to any people group in the world. Most of the ministries established during the First Wave were *by* hearing people *for* Deaf people. This was true within both denominational and nondenominational organizations.

There was an effort to develop leaders from within the Deaf community and train them for leadership but this was led primarily by hearing ministers, usually pastors with theological training or church interpreters. There are many examples of this. Dr. Harold Noe, who spent his career with Deaf Missions, first began a weekly Christian television show for Deaf people in 1961 in West Virginia. Duane King began teaching Bible classes at the Iowa School for the Deaf in 1968 and in 1970 founded Deaf Missions. Chip Green, in response to the urging of a number of young Deaf people, founded the *Tenth Coin* drama ministry in 1970 in Rochester, New York. In Oregon, the Gospel Ministries for the Deaf was established in 1971 under the direction of Bill Erickson. In 1974, Vicki Drummond and Debbie Klahn began the ministry *In His Sign* in Illinois. In Cincinnati, Ohio in 1974, The Deaf and Hard of Hearing Institute of Christian Education was begun by Cecil Bennett. All of these ministers are hearing people with a passion for the gospel and a love for the Deaf community. This pattern was also generally true in denominational offices for Deaf ministry and in local church ministries. For the most part, hearing people led denominational ministries. Rarely were First Wave ministries started and led by Deaf individuals.

It would be inaccurate to imply there were no strong Deaf ministers during this First Wave. One case in point is Reverend Carter Bearden. From 1949 until 1997, Carter served as a missionary with the Deaf community under the auspices of the North American Mission Board (previously called the Home Mission Board of the Southern Baptist Convention). He wrote or contributed to eight books. His most well-known book is, *A Handbook for Religious Interpreters for the Deaf* (Home Mission Board, 1975). Carter Bearden is a well-respected minister in Deaf-World through all three Waves. Clifford Bruffey, a contemporary of Bearden's, is another well-known and highly respected minister during this era. There were others across the denominational spectrum. However, with few exceptions, most Deaf ministries were led by hearing people with Deaf people operating in supportive roles.

Church-based—Ministers go where the people are and in this case, the Deaf were usually, in some way, connected with the residential schools. Therefore, it was common practice for the evangelical First Wave ministries to be located in some proximity to the schools for the Deaf. In a metropolitan area, usually the largest church of each major denomination would have interpreted services and some would also provide Deaf ministry. There was often more than one church in a given area with at least one sign language interpreter. The church-based ministries tended to be scattered but primarily in areas with pockets of Deaf people who were connected through the work place and were often graduates of the same Deaf schools.

There were enough Deaf people involved in church-related activities towards the end of the 1960s that multiple churches of various denominations would have Deaf ministry. It was nice for Deaf people to have choices with regards to religious instruction that was denominationally based but the bottom line was that churches were not motivated to cooperate nor were they inclined to. The Baptists could compete with the Methodists who had no connection with the Catholics or the Pentecostals. Churches tended to be more territorial because of the significant numbers of young Deaf people. Many times, Deaf people would move around within this circuit of ministries. A person may get mad at the pastor and move to another church while another may be unhappy at the second church and join the first. In the religious world, this is often referred to as "swapping sheep" and generally has negative ramifications.

Evangelical—There was an evangelical urgency about the decades of the 1960s and 1970s and the Deaf community was included. Some of this intensity may have been the result of a common belief in the evangelical community that the Second Coming of Christ was imminent and likely to occur before the new millennium. The focus of ministry during the First Wave was an effort to bring people into a saving relationship with God through Jesus Christ and to teach converts to share the gospel with others. With intense conviction about the possible Advent and final Day of Judgment, the fear of eternal damnation and the hope of eternal life were foremost in the minds of the evangelical ministers. Evangelical ministries strengthened their focus on the basic message of the gospel of Jesus Christ. As an example, the Bill Rice Ranch is a fundamentalist, evangelical ministry centered on Biblical preaching. Bill Rice Ranch summer camps for the Deaf began in 1953 and became a significant influence during the early years of the First Wave.

Interestingly, this was also a time of the developing "social gospel"[74] and general turmoil in the church in response to the changing culture. During this era, there was a huge rise of cults, humanism, atheism and other religions in America. It became evident that people were becoming confused on the unique nature of Jesus Christ and the Holy Bible. This had the effect of energizing the evangelical community to actively reach people for Christ. Ministers knew the importance of people developing a Biblical faith to guard against apostasy and backsliding.

There was a sense of trying to communicate the complete message of the Bible contained in both the Old and New Testaments. It was also early in the transition from didactic instruction to teaching through discussion groups. Some evangelicals tended to be more interested in communicating specific conversion information than on focusing on the process of developing deeper faith.

Bible-centered teaching—As was true within the hearing world, those in Deaf ministry recognized the importance of Biblical knowledge as a defense against the rapidly changing culture of the 1960s and 1970s. The Bible is Truth that transcends all cultures and languages in the world. Since reading the English language is so difficult for many Deaf people, there was a need to communicate the Bible visually. For the most part, this happened through a minister who came into the residential schools and taught the Bible in sign language. During these years, there was recognition by educators of the importance of Biblical instruction in the development of good character, citizenship and the overall instruction of a well-rounded individual.

During the First Wave, there was a strong emphasis on teaching the Bible and the development of materials for teaching the Bible to Deaf individuals. Silent Word Ministries was established in 1966 as an evangelistic outreach. One of their primary missions was producing fundamentalist Bible materials. Various denominations placed a strong emphasis on producing materials for communicating the gospel. Most residential schools had both Roman Catholic and various Protestant chaplains who taught Bible studies and led students in worship. There was a basic commitment to learning Scripture as the source of Christian maturity and stability. In 1969, the Deaf International Bible College, later to be named the Carlstrom Deaf Studies Program, was established at North Central University in Minneapolis, Minnesota as an Assembly of God ministry training program.

Technology was beginning to have an impact on First Wave Deaf ministry. With the advent of visual technology, the Bible could be taught through television, on film and eventually on video. Video technology was not commonplace and film was expensive. Desk-top printing did not exist. The mimeograph machine and the typewriter were the best that many could do. Having material typeset was expensive, slow and involved repeated visits to a professional typesetting company. Copy machines were in the early stages of development. Early copiers were slow and paper came out of the machine wet; color was added with markers. Communication and event promotion were sent by postal mail or distributed by hand. The overhead projector became one of the vital communication tools for Deaf ministry and worship, as was the flannel board. One of the greatest challenges was finding and developing visual materials for the Deaf. There were numerous ministries and few materials. There was a relatively strong market for Christian visual materials for both evangelism and Biblical instruction. Deaf ministries immediately recognized the value of low-cost videos when they became available. This became an important part of the identity of many of the Deaf ministries of that era as the market for such materials was expanding.

Preaching and signed hymns—Preaching is traditionally an important part of worship for hearing people. Even churches with a sacramental perspective of worship usually listen to a homily and Scriptures delivered by one of the priests or ministers. One person stands up front and delivers a prepared message. There is a sequential flow of thought supported by Scriptures that fit within each point of the sermon. Deaf worship during the First Wave reflected this same format. Whether in interpreted services or as separate worship, the preacher delivered the message. In seminary, we referred to it as *three points, a poem, and a prayer.*

Relatively few people are aware that hymns in the church are actually an instructional medium. Important theological concepts and stories are communicated through the words of hymns. The choruses common in many worship services today have lost the instructional aspect of hymns. During the First Wave of Deaf ministry, hymns and solos usually had a theological foundation. Naturally, the sign language interpreters sensed the importance of interpreting the music as closely as possible to the English words. This was part of the instructional value of the music. Musical signing was much more dramatic to create beauty and expression. It employed beautiful movement but primarily used English structures and initialized signs. Unfortunately, this English structure could be confusing to the Deaf participants especially when performed in dramatic gestures. Some Deaf people grew to love the majesty of signed hymns while others never developed much interest in music.

In Deaf churches, during the message itself, there is generally more interaction. The minister may ask questions, or people may ask for clarification during the sermon but the distinctive trait of the First Wave was that communication was primarily one-way, from the preacher to the people. There was urgency about a specific body of important Scriptural information that needed to be communicated. Preaching was a time for reaching out with a spiritual, and in many settings, an evangelical message. Interestingly enough, some of the Deaf churches looked like mini-models of the hearing churches. They tended to follow the same structure as seen in the hearing world. Worship music is where this was most clearly visible. It was usually comprised of favorite old hymns interpreted with and for the Deaf participants.

Inclusion with Hearing (interpreting)—The words *inclusion* and *exclusion* have opposite meanings in the Deaf-World and the hearing world. For Deaf people, there is generally a sense of *exclusion* from the hearing setting and *inclusion* is only experienced in Deaf-World. By using the word *inclusion*, I am referring to the hearing perspective of the First Wave ministries that meant inclusion in the activities of the larger, hearing Body of Christ, through interpreters. Deaf ministry was the door through which the Deaf community could access the activities of the local church and the larger fellowship of believers. There was an effort to provide interpreters as part of inclusion with the larger hearing ministry.

Inclusion with hearing people does not mean there were not separate Deaf churches. There were a number of strong Deaf churches as already described. Inclusion means there was a fundamental belief (primarily from the hearing world) that Deaf ministry was at its best when it was included with the larger, hearing worship. The hearing church had all the beautiful music, powerful preaching, and excitement of being with a large group of people. There was little understanding of the Deaf preference for a smaller, separate worship without any of the frills. Bible study was another matter because hearing people could easily understand the barriers of communication for the Deaf in a mixed-group discussion setting. This was true on both the local church and larger denominational meeting level. Hearing people viewed this as being inclusive.

"All God's Children" (Deaf are not different)—Deaf people during this era were viewed by many hearing people within the Christian faith as people who simply could not hear. There was not widespread appreciation for the unique ways Deaf individuals acquire and retain information. One of the goals of these ministries was to remove barriers that prevented full access for Deaf individuals. "All God's Children" (Deaf are not different) is a fundamental belief, from a hearing perspective, that as God's children, we are all basically the same. Individual differences are observed without full appreciation for the fundamental differences between groups of individuals as members of a cultural group. It is similar to white people saying about African-Americans, *"I don't see color, I just see the person."* On one hand, this is nice to say and believe. On the other hand, when we see people as simply *just like me* we may inadvertently define them by our own cultural standards. This can lead to pressuring people to conform to the majority culture and mores without recognizing the uniqueness of their experience as part of a minority group. The hearing perspective became one of *spiritual mainstreaming*—make everything accessible to the Deaf member. If barriers are removed, then we can join arms and celebrate our unity.

One possible example of this, within a structural system, is the history of the Lutheran denomination. Deaf missions were part of a separate board from 1896 until 1965 when it became part of the unified Board of Missions. In 1971, Deaf people established the International Lutheran Deaf Association (ILDA). Both the Deaf Mission Society and the *Deaf Lutheran* publication became part of the ILDA. The initial shift into *inclusion* reflected this perspective that Deaf people are not really different from hearing people (in 1965 during this First Wave) while the later development of the ILDA (by Deaf people) provides evidence of the shift that helped create the Second Wave with a focus on the uniqueness of ministry with Deaf people.

Across the denominational spectrum, in churches and denominational gatherings, the preference by those in authority was for providing interpreters instead of creating separate meetings. At one time, sizable groups of Deaf people would attend the general sessions of annual meetings and conferences. The hearing participants were welcoming and inspired to watch the Deaf community worship as part of the larger body of Christ. The level of Deaf participation would decrease during the coming Second Wave as more Deaf people expressed preference for separate events that were Deaf-led and communication was directly from the hands of the people up front instead of through interpreters.

Manually Signed English—For a variety of reasons, Manually Signed English (often times referred to as Pidgin Signed English or PSE) was a common style of communication during this First Wave. This is different from Signed Exact English but is still considered a form of coded English. Probably, the greatest reason for this tendency was the emphasis on the written Bible and understanding each word of Scripture. This was a time when a fair number of evangelical Christians were insistent on use of the King James Authorized Version of the Bible as the *only* acceptable translation. There was nowhere near the number of modern versions that we now have available to us. If you combine this focus on Scripture with the view of Deaf through a hearing paradigm, it is logical that the prevailing style of communication during the First Wave would have been Signed English.

In the educational arena, there was a new philosophy of Total Communication, a term coined in 1967 by Deaf educator Roy Holcomb, which is a simultaneous use of signs and speech for communication of the English language.[75] Many of the signs are initialized meaning that the signs are made while using the beginning letter of the word and sometimes adding the final letter of the word at the end of the sign. Total Communication is described as,

> "Philosophy of using every and all means to communicate with deaf children. The child is exposed to a formal sign-language system (based on English), finger spelling (manual alphabet), natural gestures, speech reading, body language, oral speech and use of amplification, and sometimes cued speech. The idea is to communicate and teach vocabulary and language in any manner that works. Total Communication strives to provide an easy, least restrictive communication method between the deaf child and his/her family, teachers and schoolmates. The child's simultaneous

use of speech and sign language is encouraged as is use of all other visual and contextual cues."[76]

Total Communication signs follow English structure. It is virtually impossible to speak in English and sign in ASL. There was also a prevailing bias against ASL in many educational systems. Naturally, the church was influenced by this signing style and it fit into the predisposition of learning English for comprehension of the Bible. ASL had not yet won widespread acceptance in the educational arena and so even the use of Signed English within First Wave ministries was a statement of support for the Deaf community in the generally hostile educational environment. In the educational arena, the battle during the 1960s and 1970s was not primarily between Signed English and ASL, but rather between proponents of strict oral communication and any form of signing at all. The book, "Deaf Like Me" by Thomas and James Spradley (1978, Gallaudet University Press) gives a painful description of this philosophical tension in the life of Lynn Spradley, Thomas' daughter, who was born in 1965.

Priority on English Comprehension—One of the objectives of First Wave ministries was to teach English comprehension for understanding Scripture as a foundation for the Christian life. The premise was that Deaf people processed information in the same way hearing people did, only it took longer to learn this language because they did not have the benefit of overhearing conversations. There was a subtle (and not so subtle) attempt to improve the literacy skills of the Deaf population to benefit Biblical study. This is not at all different from efforts to teach English to other people groups as a way for them to learn the Bible. An example of this is Gospel Ministries for the Deaf, which was established in 1971. A significant part of their ministry is instruction in "Patterned Language."[77] The goal was all about giving Deaf *"the language/education with which to gain an understanding of (Christist)...This will give them the ability to read God's Word and grow in the knowledge of Jesus Christ."[78]*

The challenge of comprehension of the gospel message began to shift from a priority on the written Bible to understanding of the Scripture in signs. Hearing people tend to be attached to the written Word so it follows that the assumption is made that Deaf people need the same attachment to Scripture memorization in English. One of the shifts that occurred during the First Wave was a progressive acceptance of Scripture seen visually through sign language as being equally inspired to reading the words on a page. There was still a sense that the most accurate translations into sign language would be those that most closely followed the English words. It was a significant realization that translating the original Greek and Hebrew directly into American Sign Language without going through English would be an equally valid translation to any written Bible. The Word of

God has the most impact on the individual in whose native language it is communicated—whether in words, signs, or even in story-telling traditions.

The ministries mentioned as part of the First Wave do not all fit each category described. There are other First Wave ministries that have been inadvertently left out. I hope the reader will forgive any oversight. These are generalizations that describe an era. This will also be true regarding Second Wave ministries. Many of these are the ministries that adapted to both the Second Wave and into the Third. They have grown and changed with the evolving Deaf-World. Many of their organizational traits have changed over the years as they have responded to cultural changes. These ministries are to be applauded and respected for their vision, consistency, and perseverance.

There are literally hundreds of other smaller, church-based First Wave ministries that no longer exist. Many of these were in churches near residential schools or in larger urban areas where Deaf people lived and worked. They were largely unable to adapt to the rapid changes of the past thirty years. The ones that survived were the ones most able to adapt without losing a sense of their fundamental calling from God. To get a sense of this dramatic change, take notice of the number of churches in your community that had Deaf ministries or interpreted services at some point in their history and compare this with how many currently have active ministries. The contrast is amazing. There is a lot of heartbreak behind the cessation of those Deaf ministries. Everything was about to change in Deaf-World as a completely new understanding of Deaf ministry emerged during the 1980s. The Second Wave was beginning to swell close behind the first and was moving quickly.

Discussion and Review

Waves THREE
Chapter 5—First WAVE

Expressions

Talk with someone who grew up during the First Wave of Deaf ministry. Ask them to describe their experience as a young person. How different is it from the common experiences of today?

Challenge

Imagine the available technology of that era. How would a Deaf person do something as simple as ordering a pizza? What about a more challenging situation such as resolving an error with the electric bill? Describe the level of dependency of Deaf people on hearing people during this era?

What are the possible pros and cons of each of the defining traits of First Wave ministries?

What are the key factors that changed in our culture to bring the First Wave of ministry to an end? What key trait did the First Wave ministries who survived seem to possess?

Scripture

"For I know the plans I have for you," declares the LORD, "plans to prosper you and not to harm you, plans to give you hope and a future. Then you will call upon me and come and pray to me, and I will listen to you." Jeremiah 29:11-12

The First Wave was a time of great hope and revival within the Deaf community. How does this Scripture affirm the hope that is found in God's love and presence despite the changes that have occurred? How does this apply to Deaf ministry today?

Application

What can we learn from the First Wave? What positive traits do we need to use in ministry during the 21st Century? What negative traits do we need to avoid in today's ministry?

How can we get some of the Deaf people who were part of the First Wave involved in reaching out to those who are in the Third Wave?

Chapter 6—Second Wave

The Second Wave came of age during a time of significant
upheaval and demand for legitimate Deaf rights.

The Second Wave of Deaf ministry arose during the 1980s and 1990s during a time of the "coming of age" of the Deaf Baby Boomers (Chapter 2). This generation of young people had all the traits of any boom generation with tremendous self-discovery, self-reliance and a passion for independence. Technology was still somewhat in its infancy and was not a defining factor of these years. If there were a central theme for the Second Wave, it would have to be self-determination and Deaf-Pride. There was a dramatic shift towards a new standard of ministry defined by the Deaf community.

Directly in the middle of these years, on July 26, 1990, President George Bush signed the Americans with Disabilities Act (ADA) into law. The ADA prohibits discrimination and ensures equal opportunity for persons with disabilities in public accommodations, transportation, employment, governmental services, and commercial facilities. It also mandated the establishment of TDD/telephone relay services as a way of creating a more accessible world.[79] Although there was discussion within the Deaf community regarding the appropriateness of the inclusion of deafness as a disability, the benefits of such legislation were unquestionable. The ADA is an attempt to create a level playing field for people with disabilities, providing full access to our society. The ADA became a rallying point for Deaf-Pride and a legitimate desire for equal opportunity. The public and private sectors were being held accountable by the federal government for creating non-discriminating workplaces, facilities, services, and businesses. It was a significant step forward for Deaf rights.

However, without question, the single defining moment of the Deaf community during these years was the *Deaf President Now* movement in March 1988. As mentioned previously, this Deaf-led uprising of Gallaudet University students led to the removal of a recently appointed, non-signing, hearing college President and the hiring of its first Deaf president, I. King Jordan, at the 124-year old university. *Deaf President Now* is a rallying cry synonymous with Deaf self-determination and empowerment.[80] This was one of the most effective and well-led student movements in the history of our country. The coordination of the movement and clarity of the demands by the students was a model of effective community organization.

Many of the academic books written during this era seem to obsess on the model of the oppressed Deaf underclass by the hearing majority. An underlying anger focused on domination by hearing people. The resentment carried over from the secular world into the religious arena. In some settings, this created a schism in Deaf ministry. Deaf-pride and rights began to sweep the Christian community as well. There was a general tension between the First and Second Waves of Deaf ministry. The Second Wave of Deaf ministry made some radical adjustments to the First Wave. At the core of Second Wave ministries was an attitude that Deaf ministries should be Deaf-led and hearing people should serve only in supportive, preferably invisible roles. At the risk of overstating the case, the approach of the First Wave ministries was slammed by the Second Wave.

A proclamation of Deaf autonomy known as "The Claggett Statement"[81] was given in 1984. It was filmed in American Sign Language without voicing. It began with a clear statement of faith in the death and resurrection of Jesus Christ. The second section expressed recognition at the variety of experiences of deafness and statement of a "common culture, a common language (ASL) and a common heritage of oppression." It continues, "Deaf people have long been shackled, often by the 'good' intentions of hearing people who haven't understood them. Deaf people lack meaningful representation and leadership in the major educational, professional, and political institutions that affect their lives. This lack "grows out of both the intentions and ignorance of the hearing people in power and the 'successfully oppressed' condition of deaf people who experience themselves as powerless and incompetent." It describes the general inadequacies of interpreters and most educational settings. The statement ends with a series of beliefs about Deaf ministry during the previous era and statement about the future of Deaf ministry.

- We believe that it is necessary to stop trying to communicate the Gospel through hearing people's eyes, through their interpretation and understanding of the Bible, through their methods. Deaf people have a right to know the Gospel in their own language, and relevant to their own context.

- We believe the American Sign Language is indeed a language—and a worthy and powerful vehicle for expressing the Gospel.

- We believe the Holy Spirit is leading all of us to work for a new day of justice for all deaf people. We believe the Holy Spirit is leading deaf people to develop indigenous forms of worship that can adequately convey the praise and the prayers of the deaf Christian community.

- We stand in solidarity with the oppressed peoples of the world. We believe that God empowers the oppressed to become free. By the act of attaining their own freedom, the oppressed can also help liberate those who have oppressed them.

- We believe that God is calling the Church to a new vision of the liberation of both deaf and hearing people. This vision is deeply rooted in the Gospel of Jesus Christ, and in an understanding of the spiritual, socioeconomic, political, and educational struggles of the deaf community.

- We believe God has given deaf people a unique perspective and unique gifts. The Body of Christ remains broken and fragmented while deaf people are separate and their gifts unknown and strange to most Christians. We believe God is calling us to wholeness.

- We commit ourselves to this vision, and trust God's Spirit to lead, to strengthen, and to empower us in this task. And we call upon deaf and hearing Christians alike to join together in this struggle toward freedom.

There is another fascinating story that illustrates the transition from First Wave to Second Wave. The details are sketchy but it was a drama performed during a national convention of Deaf ministry within a major denomination. On the stage were Deaf people, in the role of marionettes attached by strings and under control of the hearing puppeteers. The hearing people were controlling *every* movement of these Deaf Christians. Then, someone used a Bible to symbolically cut the strings and release the Deaf individuals to stand independently and assume control of their own lives and ministries. This proved to be a powerful, symbolic statement of the desire for Deaf-led ministry. It was a statement for Deaf autonomy, identity and respect. The drama was also fairly controversial and stirred up intense conversation about the proper role of hearing people in Deaf ministry.

Marshall Lawrence, of Silent Blessings ministry, identifies a tendency for some older ministries to have what is termed a "benevolence outreach" which may be motivated by pity. This form of outreach is ineffective and may even be harmful. He points out that we should use a "foreign missions…cross cultural outreach." Deaf language and culture are recognized and supported. Deaf leaders are nurtured and empowered.[82] This criticism is especially focused in local church ministries that were traditionally run by interpreters. The call includes autonomous Deaf churches with a focus on the cultural aspects of ministry.

When a set of three waves rolls in the ocean towards the shore, the second one is usually slightly bigger than the first. This serves as a natural example of what occurred during the Second Wave of Deaf ministry. It was an exciting time of strong Deaf-led ministries and strong Deaf leaders emerging within hearing-led ministries. Various Deaf ministry training programs and a number of Deaf churches were established. At the same time, it was a difficult transition from the First Wave to the Second Wave and there are those who were hurt in the process. Some who had been leaders during the First Wave were under fire. Interpreters in many local churches were unsure as to their proper role within the Deaf ministries that they may have even started themselves. The Second Wave was an intense time of discovery for a baby-boom generation of Deaf young people who were growing and assuming new God-given rights. Expectations were high in both secular and religious settings for a new day of powerful Deaf Culture ministries.

Defining traits of the Second Wave
2nd Wave
1980s and 1990s

Team leadership
Deaf-led
Revival and traveling ministries
Instructional
Cultural Awareness and Fellowship
Focus on drama
Indigenous Deaf churches
Deaf identity and rights (We are unique)
American Sign Language
Priority on Teaching ASL skills and Deaf Culture

Team leadership—Team leadership is an important part of Deaf culture that provides a model of decision-making that includes everyone in the group involved in the final decision. It is a more *communal* identity rather than just one person arbitrarily making choices for other people. This is partially in reaction to the autocratic models of decision-making Deaf people experience in the hearing world. People who have experienced a sense of victimization tend to be more sensitive in how decisions are being made by those in authority. One of the strengths of the Second Wave was an effort to build ministry programs based on the needs expressed by the members of the group being served. This reflects the priority of teaching young Deaf people to think independently and avoid being controlled by others, particularly by hearing people.

One interesting example of the shift from individual and team leadership was in the process of the translation of the Bible into ASL (called the Omega Project) under the auspices of Deaf Missions in Council Bluffs, Iowa. When the project began in 1981, the burden of translation was basically on one person. The first four tapes of the series reflected a more signed English format. In 1985-1986, there was a conscious shift to a team approach for making the translation. Deaf people were involved in all aspects of the process. The signing style became definitively ASL and the quality of the finished product reflected the benefits of a shift into a team leadership model.[83]

A communal model of decision-making has both strengths and weaknesses. It reflects the Scriptural model of gifts of the Body of Christ and a heart of service to one another. It brings out untapped leadership skill and creates an environment of personal discovery and enlightenment. There is a downside; team-led ministries can become obsessed on the relationships within the team to the neglect of those being served. It can become divisive and combative. The team can lose productivity in the effort to get everyone on-board with decisions. It can become a seedbed of discontent and power struggles. All in all though, the team-led model is one of the notably positive characteristics of Second Wave ministries. God uses the diverse perspectives of a team of participants most fully to express Himself and His leadership.

Deaf-led—One of the defining trademarks of this era was an insistence on having the ministry led by Deaf people whether or not they were the person paid to lead the ministry. In other words, hearing people could be part of the ministry but must take a back seat to the opinions, needs, and wants of the Deaf leadership. This made for some frustrating relationships but ultimately was a statement of Deaf self-determination and empowerment. It was a great opportunity for the Deaf leadership to build skills and earn respect as capable ministers and leaders. This type of indigenous leadership tends to be more tuned-in to the cultural needs of young Deaf people. The language skills and understanding of the cultural experience of deafness is virtually impossible for hearing people to grasp fully. The role model and relationship provided by Deaf leadership is vital for the *transference of faith* from one generation to the next, through positive relationships and interactions with other, older Deaf people of faith.

This desire for Deaf-led ministries had the potential to evolve into a resistance of any hearing leadership in Deaf ministry other than those who served as interpreters. At a workshop I attended a few years ago, a Deaf minister made the statement that *"hearing ministers used to lead and the Deaf would follow; now, we need the Deaf ministers to lead and the hearing should follow. We need you to get out of the way and let us lead."* This is a classic Second Wave perspective. Another volunteer leader once asked me about a summer camp for Deaf teenagers, *"Who will the interpreters be at the camp?"* I explained that we have no interpreters; only signing leaders, Deaf and Hearing, who will be ministering with the teens. This perspective puzzled him because he understood ministry through the Second Wave paradigm where hearing people were simply tolerated because of the need for interpreters. If no interpreters were needed, then hearing people were not particularly welcomed. At times, this created an unpleasant environment and an undercurrent of discontent and strained relationships.

Revival and traveling ministries—A common characteristic of the Second Wave ministries was the traveling revival model of ministry. Many of the Deaf ministries during this time were connected with the residential schools; however, more and more Deaf children were becoming mainstreamed and scattered. In response, it became important for ministries to be transportable and to travel for workshops, revival services and camps. The Deaf church was still vibrant and many hearing churches had active Deaf ministries. Part of the mission of these ministries was to bring awareness of Deaf culture and identity to places other than just the areas around the residential schools.

Deaf Opportunity Outreach (DOOR) and Tenth Coin are excellent examples of traveling ministries during this era. DOOR began as a local church outreach in 1983 and expanded to become an international ministry. During the Second Wave, they provided music, drama, and summer camps. At one point, Tenth Coin had several traveling ministries that traversed the country and met annually in Louisville, Kentucky—called the "Festival of Choirs"—for a time of renewal and refreshment.[84] There were other traveling drama/music teams but these two in particular had a tremendous impact across the country during the early years of the Second Wave.

Deaf Worldwide Ministries, another Deaf-led ministry, began a traveling ministry drama group in 1990 called the "Master's Hands" for this purpose. Visual Effects, from North Georgia, began during the late 1980s. Silent Touch was a music ministry team from Texas, also popular during this era. This list is nowhere near exhaustive but gives you some idea of the number of traveling, revival Deaf Drama/Music groups during the Second Wave. Signing became such a popular expression of worship and music that some traveling groups existed from local churches that were hearing people who would use signing as part of the musical presentation but did not know sign language. As one might imagine, this would present quite a shock to a Deaf participant who wanted to chat with the signing choir following the worship service!

Instructional—Deaf Missions lead in the process of translating the Bible in American Sign Language, called the Omega Project, in 1982 under the leadership of Dr. Harold Noe. Deaf Video Communications in Chicago, Illinois was established in 1983 with a strong emphasis on producing visuals for effective ways to communicate the gospel. Many of the First Wave ministries also began providing more instruction and training for Deaf people involved in Deaf ministry. There was a basic transition of ministry training between the First and Second Waves; instead of training hearing people on how to do Deaf ministry, there was a strong shift to instructing an indigenous leadership.

In 1989, Gary Barrett, a Deaf minister from Oklahoma, began Deaf Worldwide Ministries (DWM). The mission of DWM is to bring the gospel of Jesus Christ to the Deaf community around the world. They established a Deaf evangelism training center in Sulphur, Oklahoma. They also offer ordination and licensing for Deaf ministers and those involved in Deaf ministry.

There were a number of ministry training programs established for Deaf individuals during this time. The Deaf Program at Boyce Bible School in Louisville, Kentucky began in the fall of 1989 after DOOR moved their headquarters to the area. The first students were from DOOR. The headquarters for DOOR remained in Louisville for five years and then moved. The enrollment decreased after they left and Boyce closed the school in the mid-1990s.

In 1995, the Southern Baptist replaced the Boyce program with the Tri-State Minister Training program based in North Carolina. This program allowed students to live and minister in different areas and come together for training. Students receive credit from Gardner-Webb University in North Carolina for coursework. This is another indication of the scattering of the Deaf community that was occurring as we move into the early years of the Third Wave and the modifications that are necessary to provide accessible and effective religious training for the Deaf community.

There are other examples of Second Wave ministries whose mission was to train Deaf ministry leadership that came into existence towards the end of the Second Wave. Harvest Deaf Bible College in Ringgold, Georgia was established in 1996 with twelve students and had its first graduating class in 2003. Capital Baptist Deaf College, a ministry of Hampshire View Deaf Baptist Church in Silver Spring, Maryland graduated its first four students in 2003. Both of these examples are Deaf-led ministries with a commitment on training Deaf ministers. Instruction is a constant between each of the waves; however, the Second Wave incorporated a much stronger emphasis on understanding oneself as part of Deaf culture and primarily (or exclusively) training Deaf individuals for ministry.

Cultural Awareness and Fellowship—Because the Deaf community was becoming aware of the rapidly changing scenario in our country (which ultimately became the Deaf Diaspora) and the dangers presented to the very existence of the Deaf community, much of the mission of Second Wave ministries was on maintaining and protecting Deaf identity and culture. Some of the ministries provided sporting and social activities for the purpose of building a connection between the scattered children and the culturally Deaf adults. The first step was creating cultural awareness. In many places you will see it expressed as "Deaf Culture Ministry" or see a distinction made as a d/Deaf ministry. The little "d" refers to those who cannot hear but have no real connection with the traditional Deaf culture and the capital "D" refers to those who chose to be part of the community. Deaf people were invited to participate as part of a cultural group and then led into Christian maturity as a Deaf person.

The Deaf Club is a vital part of Deaf-World. In most places, it is an exclusive place to gather with other Deaf people for social interaction. During the 1990s, some of these clubs became less family friendly and more like a bar than a church social. The intuition of those in the Christian faith was to emphasize the positive social interactions within the church that avoided many negative influences. Second Wave ministries recognized the importance of Deaf culture socialization as they explored new ways to create positive settings for this interaction to occur. In a world where one feels controlled and oppressed from an outside group, the tendency is to respond with unstructured settings that simply allow for social interaction. Cultural awareness and fellowship became an important characteristic of Second Wave ministries.

Focus on drama—There is widespread consensus that drama is the most effective means of communication of the gospel to the Deaf-Mind. Most Deaf people thoroughly enjoy watching dramatic stories expressed in sign language. Stories expressed in drama became identified as the most effective way for Deaf individuals to understand and retain the information in a spiritual message. Second Wave dramas were not necessarily Bible narratives and verses; rather, symbolic stories of the Creation or the struggle of good and evil in one's life. One's personal temptation in a world full of peril is a common theme. There would later be a return to direct communication of Biblical stories but during this era was a desire for practical encouragement through drama for facing daily challenges.

During the early years of the Second Wave, there was still a strong connection with music. Much of the worship included traditional and contemporary music of that time. Mark Mitchum is one of the most famous performers of that era and his unique style involved a blend of drama and music; actually a dramatic interpretation of music. His beautiful signing of Christian music attracted both hearing and Deaf audiences.[85] Oftentimes, it was an entire choir of signers who would communicate the message of the music in dramatic form as a unit based on movement and positions. It possessed a dance-like element that was flowing and visually pleasing. In some more conservative church settings, this was frowned upon because of the association with dance.

The ministry of the Deaf drama/music group, the Tenth Coin, was one of the visionary influences in the transition from First Wave to Second Wave. Chip

Green, founder of the ministry, realized the disabling influence and patronizing relationship created by the hearing leadership of Deaf ministry. Although Tenth Coin began in 1970, during the First Wave and initially reflected many First Wave traits, it was very influential in the movement into the Second Wave and became a strong Second Wave ministry. One of the priorities became the development of strong, competent voice-interpreters to communicate effectively the thoughts and insights of the truly Deaf leadership. The ministry of Tenth Coin was primarily designed to minister to the group of young Deaf people within the group and help them develop ministry, relationship, and leadership skills. The traveling drama/music part of the ministry was an opportunity for these young people to experience a growth producing environment through ministry. The priority was on the personal maturing of young Deaf people into fully committed followers of Christ.

During the later years of the Second Wave, music became identified as a "hearing" experience and some ministries began to perform Deaf drama without music. There was a shift in both the Deaf churches and ministries of the Second Wave away from traditional hymns and music in general. Music holds little appeal for some people in the Deaf community. More radical elements maintain that hearing people invented music for themselves and the *true* Deaf have no interest in music. This created an uncomfortable relationship with many of the hearing people involved in Deaf ministry because of the love for music by hearing people as part of worship. For some, hearing and Deaf, rejection of music became a badge of true commitment to Deaf-World. For other Deaf people, music continues to be a source of enjoyment and inspiration.

Indigenous Deaf churches—During the Second Wave, there was a logical move towards Deaf churches that were chartered as distinct, self-sufficient organizations. Worship was in ASL and the essential leadership of the church were Deaf and hard of hearing members. Hearing people may have participated but would need to accept a supportive role only. Even if the Deaf church was not fully separate from the sponsoring church, there was a movement to have the gospel presented directly from the hands of a signing minister and not through an interpreter. Voice interpreting was offered for the signing-impaired.

Many of these churches reflected the traditions of the past with hymns, offerings, ushers, announcements, Scripture-reading, and a sermon. There was an emphasis on the socialization aspects of church such as picnics and covered-dish fellowships. There were clearly some distinctive Deaf cultural traits such as the use of a chalkboard or overhead projector and interaction with the congregation during the message. However, it was not a radical departure from the traditions of the hearing church. One of the major issues faced by the Deaf church was how to serve the hearing children, parents, and siblings of the Deaf church members.

Because of the relatively large numbers of Deaf people during this era, churches continued to grow in spite of this difficulty.

The chaplains at the residential schools for the Deaf were dramatically affected by the overall changes in the educational system. Between the double impact of Deaf students traveling home every weekend (not staying at the residential schools over the weekends) and the secularization of the educational setting, the role of the chaplain became almost obliterated. There was a general rejection by the school system of the chaplain as a legitimate part of the residential school. The chaplains were a primary link to separate Deaf worship and this was a huge loss to the local Deaf churches and ministries across the spectrum.

Deaf identity & rights (We are unique)—Deaf people during this era began to reassert themselves as individuals who were not looking to the hearing world for self-definition. The community was empowered and liberated from any earlier dependency on their hearing counterparts for affirmation. They recognized the uniqueness and exclusivity of being Deaf. A Deaf person's experience with God was uniquely Deaf and not truly understandable by hearing people. What was desired was the recognition of the Deaf culture and rights of the Deaf individual. Deaf ministry began to advocate for Deaf issues, concerns and preferences.

One of the best examples of the blend of the Christian faith and the importance of Deaf culture during the Second Wave is found in the *Ten Commandments of Deaf Culture*. This is included in the information about the Deaf Worldwide Ministries and targets, "the non-Deaf (missionary, pastor, evangelist, interpreter, etc.) while in the presence of a Deaf person."

I.   You shall not put "Hearing Culture" above Deaf Culture.

II. You shall not lose eye contact when communicating.

III. You shall communicate in sign language at all times.

IV. You shall not be the Deaf person's sign language teacher.

V.   You shall not be the Deaf person's English grammar teacher.

VI. You shall not be the Deaf person's speech therapist.

V.   You shall not tell non-Deaf jokes and puns.

VI. You shall not be the Deaf person's "mother."

IX. You shall view Deaf as an ethnic group, not as handicapped.

X.   You shall believe Deaf can do all things through Christ.[86]

During the Second Wave, cultural sensitivity became central to effective ministry. Part of reaching Deaf people with the gospel was to avoid the patronizing tendency of hearing people who are oblivious to deafness as an identifiable cultural and language group. To reach a cultural group with the gospel requires recognizing the mores and social nuances of personal interactions within the community.

American Sign Language—American Sign Language became the litmus test for those involved with Second Wave ministries. Signing in English signs and structures was seen as an assault on the integrity and legitimacy of ASL as the natural language of the Deaf. There was little accommodation for the Deaf/Oral individuals and a general bias against them as a group of people who rejected their deafness; who wanted to be "hearing." Occasionally, this translated into a tension between the Deaf role models and the Deaf person's hearing family and friends. Many hearing families felt threatened by this dynamic and felt insecure about sending their children into Deaf environments for fear their children would lose their emotional connections with home. The ministries may have had no intention of disrupting the family unit but because of the absence of hearing people within these ministries, many times, there was a fundamental lack of trust by the hearing parents of Deaf children.

The positioning of ASL as the primary means of communicating the gospel is a tremendous strength of the Second Wave. The gospel communicated in ASL has much more power and impact to the Deaf-Mind than filtering it through the English language. The advent of Chronological Bible Storying in the Deaf-World became a way to use strong ASL skills and Bible drama to teach Scripture.[87] There was also a visible change in the video resources during this time from Manually Signed English to American Sign Language. This is seen in the ongoing development of *The Bible: ASL Translation* by Deaf Missions. They actually went back and rerecorded earlier signed English versions to create a consistent ASL translation of the Bible.

Priority on teaching ASL skills and Deaf Culture—Teaching American Sign Language skills with a focus on maintaining Deaf culture became paramount during the Second Wave. Part of the distinctiveness of Deaf ministry is the unique experience of growing up Deaf. The church became an important place for keeping Deaf culture alive and teaching Deaf cultural values. Many hearing people who came into ministry during this era were baptized into Deaf-World as the door into Deaf ministry. For some, there was a sense of *we are a new generation of hearing ministers with the Deaf who avoid the traps of earlier patronizing ministries. We understand our role as simply facilitators and supporters.* A fundamental commitment to the traditional values of the Deaf community and the priority on ASL and Deaf culture was required for full participation in the ministry.

Scriptural and practical truths were taught but a priority became instruction about the cultural Deaf-World. The priority of First Wave ministries was building English skills and comprehension. The Second Wave ministries were basically unconcerned with teaching English skills at all. Signed English was considered the language of the oppressor; ASL is the native language of the Deaf people. The philosophical foundation of the Second Wave was one of developing a Deaf identity as competent adults on equal footing with those in the hearing world. Being Deaf is not a second-class citizenship in the Kingdom of God. The fundamental building block for a strong Christian faith was recognition of one's rights and self-determination as a Deaf person. Hearing authority was viewed as shackles to be thrown off. The priority became maintaining a sense of Deaf pride that created personal confidence, success, and spirituality.

The descriptions of Second Wave ministries are generalizations that describe an era. Some of these ministries are now adapting into the Third Wave. As God is breathing revival into the Deaf community, these Second Wave individuals and ministries may be the key to the effectiveness of Deaf ministry during the new century. Those who are able to respond to the New Culture of Deafness without losing sense of the traditional culture of Deafness will have the greatest impact on the spread of the gospel into the lives of the next generation of Deaf and hard of hearing children and youth. Many of those whose lives were touched by the gospel during the Second Wave are returning to the fold. Many who have been battered and bruised by the secular assault on Christianity during the past twenty years are returning to faith. This creates a vital strength and link to generations past. The "Missing Generation" is being found and brought to faith in Christ.

Probably the best example of a Second Wave ministry is Deaf Opportunity Outreach (DOOR). I recommend visiting their website at www.doorinternational.com and studying it carefully to understand the values and perspectives of the Second Wave ministries. Although headquartered in the United States, they are now almost exclusively in other countries. They offer a one-year training program exclusively for people who are Deaf and hard of hearing. They will not train hearing people for Deaf ministry unless that person happens to be the spouse of a Deaf person called to ministry. They focus solely on the establishment of indigenous Deaf churches. They have a deep commitment to exclusively Deaf leadership of Deaf people. They currently have ministry training centers in Kenya, Hungary, Costa Rica, Philippines and India.[88]

The Second Wave of Deaf ministry brought many positive insights that were of great benefit to evangelical ministry. In fact, if the Deaf Diaspora had not occurred (the community had remained centralized) the Second Wave would have ultimately carried the day. I believe this is why many Second Wave ministries are focusing their efforts on missions in other countries. Those foreign mission fields are much more like the United States of the early 20th Century. The Deaf in Third World countries are generally gathered in centralized locations and not scattered as they are in the United States. The Deaf Diaspora in our country is unique and presents challenges that Second Wave ministries cannot overcome without adapting.

Those who cannot adjust to the changes brought about by the Deaf Diaspora will continued to be puzzled by the teenagers described at the end of Chapter 4. Ministry involves reaching people where they are and helping them mature into what God wants them to be. In the next section, suggestions for reaching this next generation, this New Culture of Deafness, will be given in an attempt to pull from the best of the First and Second Waves. The underpinnings of the Second Wave are vital but must be open to how to connect with Deaf young people who now grow up in a world radically different from any generation in the history of Deaf-World. It is an exciting opportunity for intergenerational, intercultural partnerships to recapture the spiritual center of Deaf-World as a vital part of experiencing a meaningful life.

Discussion and Review

Waves THREE
Chapter 6—Second WAVE

Expressions

Talk with someone who grew up during the Second Wave of Deaf ministry. Ask them to describe their experience as a teenagers and young adult. How different is it from the common experiences of Deaf teenagers today?

Challenge

Visit the DOOR website on the internet at *www.doorinternational.com*. Identify as many traits of the Second Wave as you can find. Discuss the pros and cons of these traits in both the foreign mission setting and also in the United States.

One of the marks of the Second Wave was a strong bias toward "Only Deaf minister to Deaf" and a resistance to hearing-led ministers as being "patronizing" or "controlling" of the Deaf. What is your opinion of this issue? Explain both sides of the issue.

Scripture

"You used to be far from God. Your thoughts made you his enemies, and you did evil things. But his Son became a human and died. So God made peace with you, and now he lets you stand in his presence as people who are holy and faultless and innocent. But you must stay deeply rooted and firm in your faith. You must not give up the hope you received when you heard the good news. It was preached to everyone on earth, and I myself have become a servant of this message." Colossians 1:21-23

The Second Wave was a time of transition to Deaf-led ministry. The gospel is eternal and applies to every generation, although the format may change. How were these truths applied during the Second Wave? How did these ministries adapt to the impact of the Deaf Diaspora?

Application

What positive traits do we need to use in ministry during the 21st Century? What negative traits do we need to avoid in today's ministry? What challenges are there for those who are part of the Second Wave in reaching out to the Third Wave Deaf? What can we learn from the Second Wave?

Chapter 7—Third Wave

The Third Wave brings hope to the future of Deaf ministry. God uses the gifts and unity of his people to reach a scattered population.

We stand at the beginning of the Third Wave of Deaf ministry as we enter the 21st Century. This book is designed to articulate the anticipated traits of the Third Wave and provide a model for effective ministry for this next generation. If the Deaf community is to overcome the secularization of Deaf-World and reclaim their rightful place as a community of historic and significant faith, we must focus our energy on the generation that is coming of age during the new millennium. Most of the rest of this book will address ministry with young people who became teenagers after the turn of the 20th Century.

There are many Deaf and hard of hearing people whose primary cultural experience is remarkably similar to that of their hearing peers. With changes in our culture becoming more inclusive and accessible, and the improvement of technology, many Deaf people are simply part of the mainstream fabric of America. One of the questions often asked is, *"Where are the Deaf Baby Boomers now? If there is a large population of Deaf people who were born in the middle 1960s, where are they now?"*

Deaf people are scattered, and for the most part, are not connected with church. Many Deaf people born in the 1960s and 1970s are working, raising children and beginning to recognize the importance of spiritual influence in their families. Some are starting to return to church. The Third Wave of Deaf ministry requires a willingness to cooperate across denominational lines in a post-modern world. We need to reach out to them in ways which they can relate. We cannot try the same old things and expect different results. The church cannot just wait for them to return. We must actively find them and respond to their needs.

Returning to the similarities with the African-American community, there are those who have a clearly distinctive cultural and language experience (therefore having to function as bilingual and bicultural) yet there is also a significant population of African-Americans whose primary cultural experiences are not unlike the majority white population. They live in a blended culture that *is* mainstream America. They live in integrated neighborhoods, go to integrated schools and workplaces, and enjoy friendships with people of diverse backgrounds. They are still proudly African-Americans and enjoy their heritage, folkways, mores, and cultural preferences, but their day-to-day cultural experience is not remarkably different from others who are Caucasian. They are part of a larger blended "American" culture yet are included as part of an identifiable sub-group within the culture. They are not truly bilingual/bicultural but are simply an identifiable part of the fabric of society.

Since the Third Wave is just beginning, this section is designed to provide a blueprint for effective ministry based on what has been observed from the first two waves. It is also a recommendation based on what has been effective since the establishment of DeafYouth Ministries in 2000. In the fullness of time, DeafYouth Ministries/DTQuest was incorporated to bring together the best wisdom from Deaf ministry and youth ministry to reach the scattered population of Deaf and hard of hearing teenagers. To the best of our knowledge, DeafYouth Ministries/DTQuest is the only national, interdenominational ministry specifically designed for Deaf and hard of hearing teenagers.

The hearing world of youth ministry has been dealing with the effects of reaching scattered, secular populations over the last half of the 20th Century. Organizations like Youth Specialties and more recently, the National Network of Youth Ministers have been responding to the changing dynamics of our culture through training for many years.[89] Desegregation of public schools during the 1970s and busing of students led to a similar scattering of people within the same neighborhoods and communities. In any metropolitan area, the average youth group in a church has students in a number of different schools so they are serving a scattered population as well. Young Life and Youth For Christ have been reaching out to unchurched and non-Christian teenagers for more than half a century.[90] We can learn a great deal from these ministries and other groups as well.

Remember our fictional youth group described at the end of Chapter 4? There was Aleah, Brian, Christina, Deon, Erica, Federico, and Gracie representing a wide range of ages, educational environments and communication preferences. They are diverse, scattered and most have little Biblical knowledge or concern with spiritual matters. We have to think differently about how to reach people during the Deaf Diaspora. We must recognize the distinctive traits of this New Culture of Deafness.

In the next section, we deal with more specific information about ministry with young people as diverse as the one described. This chapter addresses the distinctive traits of the Third Wave based on the strengths of both the First and Second Waves. You may note a change in writing style that is more anecdotal and informal. The ten traits follow the same format used in evaluating the first two waves and are important markers for effective ministry. By being intentional, we are able to participate in the revival God has begun across the country to reach Deaf people with the hope found only in Jesus Christ as personal Lord and Savior.

Defining Traits of The Third Wave
3rd Wave
2000s and 2010s

> Individual and team leadership
> Gifts—diversity and unity
> Large geographical regions
> Importance of missions
> Outreach and relational ministry
> Technology, drama, Deaf-music, basic Gospel
> Inclusive and unique programming
> Equal access to the Gospel
> ASL with acceptance of other communications styles
> Priority on personal relationships

Individual and team leadership—Jesus modeled this blend of individual and team leadership for us. Some have a gift for leadership and are called to lead. All are called to use their gifts for ministry. A team needs leadership; a leader needs a team. Excellence occurs when someone, *who has a servant's heart,* leads a team of people who are diverse yet unified by the spirit of Jesus Christ. God has created us to work as part of a body of believers. Read the advice given to Moses by his father-in-law in Exodus 15. Study carefully the 12th Chapters of both Romans and 1st Corinthians. Read the final chapters of John. Read the whole New Testament. We are foolish to ignore the importance of ministry based on gifts from God.

The Scripture says it best:

> *"Now the body is not made up of one part but of many. If the foot should say, 'Because I am not a hand, I do not belong to the body,' it would not for that reason cease to be part of the body. And if the ear should say, 'Because I am not an eye, I do not belong to the body,' it would not for that reason cease to be part of the body. If the whole body were an eye, where would the sense of hearing be? If the whole body were an ear, where would the sense of smell be? But in fact God has arranged the parts in the body, every one of them, just as he wanted them to be. If they were all one part, where would the body*

be? As it is, there are many parts, but one body. The eye cannot say to the hand, 'I don't need you!' And the head cannot say to the feet, 'I don't need you!' On the contrary, those parts of the body that seem to be weaker are indispensable, and the parts that we think are less honorable we treat with special honor. And the parts that are unpresentable are treated with special modesty, while our presentable parts need no special treatment. But God has combined the members of the body and has given greater honor to the parts that lacked it, so that there should be no division in the body, but that its parts should have equal concern for each other. If one part suffers, every part suffers with it; if one part is honored, every part rejoices with it. Now you are the body of Christ, and each one of you is a part of it." (1 Corinthians 12:14-27, NIV).

Sustainable ministry uses both individual and team decision-making processes. One must lead a team with full recognition that Christ is the true "head" of the "body" (Ephesians 1:22-23). The leader must follow Jesus' example of servant leadership by washing the feet of the disciples and sending them out to serve God (John 13:1-17). In the past, ministries would "pop-up/pop-down;" they would exist for only a short period of time and would disappear when the leader moved or burned-out. Teenagers need to have dependable influences in their lives. Using a team creates stability. A team has insights that no single person could possibly have; *we* are smarter than any *one* of us.

For Third Wave ministries to be effective, someone must steer the boat with great sensitivity to those in the boat, including those with a gift for navigation. It is ideal when this person is also Deaf because of the role model this provides for Deaf youth. The key qualifier is to have a gift for leadership and a call from God. However, for this new generation of Deaf teenagers, being deaf is not a requirement to lead this ministry although the team leader must have fluency in American Sign Language. She or he must be comfortable working with a wide variety of people from various cultural backgrounds and communication styles.

Gifts—diversity and unity—It is vital for a ministry team to be diverse and unified. Unity *without* diversity will not reach the variety of Deaf teens in today's world; diversity *without* unity is a formula for disaster. The team must be built upon the gifts of the Body, not whether someone is Deaf or not, or signs in only ASL or not. The ideal team is a blend of people who love Jesus and each other; who are black, brown, white; young, middle, old; Deaf, hard of hearing, hearing; and come from a variety of denominational backgrounds. This is one of the areas where Third Wave ministries distinguish themselves from the Second Wave; they pursue diversity in leadership that includes hearing people. The two vital words to remember for successful Third Wave ministries are *diversity* and *unity*. We need as diverse a ministry team as possible (of Biblically committed Christians) who love each other deeply and sincerely.

The team must develop a sense of commitment to each other and respect for differences in perspectives, skills, denominations, and personal gifts. Young Deaf people need to see Deaf adults working side-by-side with hearing adults as Christians. Why are hearing people important? One reason is because these young Deaf people will be interacting with hearing people throughout their lives as brothers and sisters in Christ. Most are from hearing families. They need to see Deaf and hearing adults working as co-laborers for the Kingdom of God. This prepares these young people for their rightful place as full participants in service to Christ as peers and equals to hearing people. The Bible says the world will recognize we are followers of Christ in how we love each other. We are the Body of Christ. We are one in the Spirit.

There is an exercise we do in workshops in which we choose a large male in the group to lie down on a table. We select the smallest female in the room and ask her to pick him up. Of course, she cannot and is often frustrated.

"What happens if you try?" I ask.

"I will hurt myself and maybe drop him" is the common reply.

"But it is your responsibility to pick him up. How are you going to do this?"

Eventually she figures out to *ask for help* from the rest of the group. The group surrounds the individual and easily lifts him. In fact, we have each person use only their index finger on both hands and to everyone's surprise, the group still easily lifts him. The point is that by working as a team, we can have a greater impact and create a sustainable ministry. It is not exhausting when you work together.

There are some other practical reasons as well. A young hard of hearing leader who grew up Deaf-Oral or has a signed-English background will be able to connect with teens who are currently mainstreamed and have a similar experience. A Second Wave, Deaf leader with strong ASL skills and background in the traditional Deaf culture can have a tremendous impact on teens from residential settings and especially those who have Deaf parents. They also bring credibility to the ministry within the Deaf community. An older Deaf leader who grew up during the First Wave brings wisdom, maturity and often has a deep knowledge of the Bible. A hearing, middle-aged member of the team who has a Deaf teenage child will be able to more easily connect with the hearing parents of the teenagers. This creates trust with the parents. A young, single leader with energy and a flexible schedule can hang out with the teens at sporting events. The strength of the team is with Christ at the head and an attitude of love and acceptance of each other and the different gifts of the body.

Large geographic regions—A famous quote is attributed to a bank robber named Willie Sutton *(although Sutton gives credit to the creativity of the newspaper reporter who interviewed him)*; when asked, "Why do you rob banks, Willie?" he responded with, *"Because that's where the money is."[91]* The reality of ministry is you must go *where the people are* and now, in today's world, this is the first challenge of Deaf ministry. We must find the people.

There are still a significant number of Deaf students attending residential schools. Due to the changing demographics, the numbers have decreased over the past three decades and a significantly higher percentage of the students at the schools for the Deaf have physical and/or emotional problems. Third Wave ministries must now think in terms of ministry to teenagers in residential schools but primarily in large geographic regions and across denominations. We even have to work across para-church organizations. No one can do it alone but we can reach Deaf teenagers by working together. Part of the ministry is finding ways to overcome the problems created by distance and differences. It is important to maintain and strengthen the natural supports in their lives such as the family, church, and neighborhood. The teens gather together to learn and grow but return to their own worlds to apply what they have experienced.

One of the reasons for building a diverse leadership team is to have people who can connect with teenagers from multi-educational settings. Effective ministry is intentional in meeting the relational and spiritual needs of every Deaf and hard of hearing teenager, and tailors the programming to the group. This balanced and widespread approach is part of what attracts the teenagers to the events. It is their desire to meet other teenagers who are Deaf. Gathering together with teens from other environments helps to expand their worlds and creates a new connection between teens of differing experiences within the Deaf community. Ignoring one group to serve the other loses some of the vitality of diversity and large numbers which teens enjoy.

There is a general suspicion by some of the word "ecumenical," because it is seen as a weakening of the gospel. Ecumenical is a positive word that simply means, "relating to the worldwide Christian church; concerned with establishing unity with and among churches."[92] There is not a losing of theological identity within denominations; there is a building of unity based around that with which all agree. Most major denominations have primary beliefs (the core gospel of personal salvation only through Jesus' death and resurrection and some combination of God's grace, personal faith, and good works) and then have various issues that separate them from others, such as view of the Eucharist (Lord's Supper), mode and meaning of baptism, eternal security, role of woman in ministry, the gift of tongues, structure of church authority, and other issues. These are denominational issues that are important to those within that church. Historically, these types of issues were such a focus that it kept the Body of Christ divided, and at least politely disconnected.

The Third Wave can accurately be described as a *post-denominational* movement meaning the labels that separate us are not nearly as important as the Spirit who unites us. To be post-denominational means we still treasure our traditions and recognize our differences but realize that Deaf teenagers who have no knowledge of Jesus Christ are not interested in theological discourse. They want to know how to fill this emptiness in their hearts. They are separate from God by sin and need to know of God's great provision of grace and forgiveness through Jesus Christ. They need to know, *"For he has rescued us from the dominion of darkness and brought us into the kingdom of the Son He loves, in whom we have redemption, the forgiveness of sins."* (Colossians 1:13-14) Deaf teenagers are so scattered that no individual denomination, church, para-church ministry (i.e. Young Life, Youth For Christ, Fellowship of Christian Athletes, Campus Crusade for Christ), or Deaf ministry can reach them all. We must be willing to maintain our unique identities while recognizing that this is a post-denominational generation in need of a relationship with Jesus Christ. A common saying to make this point is, "The main thing is to keep the Main thing the main thing."

The largest numbers of Deaf teenagers are found in two places. They tend live in large metropolitan areas in the mainstreamed educational settings (unless the school for the Deaf is actually in that urban setting) or they attend the residential school for the Deaf and live scattered across the state. This creates a new challenge. The average Deaf teenager in a mainstreamed setting and the average Deaf teenager in the residential setting have two completely different experiences of deafness. Third Wave ministry must adapt to these differences and use it as a positive strength for reaching all Deaf teenagers with the gospel. There are hundreds of other Deaf and hard of hearing children who are scattered across the state and may be the only Deaf child mainstreamed in the entire county. We hear stories of isolated Deaf children thinking they will either become hearing or die before growing up because they did not realize there was such a thing as a Deaf adult. The most effective ministry covers large geographical areas. It connects the residential schools as a hub for statewide ministry with a focus on the metropolitan areas.

Missions—Originally, this section was going to focus on evangelism *and* instruction; basically key traits from the First and Second Waves. Third Wave ministry requires both. After further reflection and observation, I believe that involvement of Deaf teenagers in mission opportunities is the one of the most vital characteristics of Third Wave ministry. *Missions* incorporates both evangelism and discipleship. Involving Deaf teens in missions is a critical part of reaching teens for Christ, instructing them towards maturity of faith and creating a permanent connection with Christianity for a lifetime. A Third Wave ministry without missions will fall short of developing fully devoted followers of Christ.

In the residential setting, there are many opportunities for students to develop leadership skills. This is seldom the case in the mainstreamed setting. The bulk of mainstreamed Deaf students have few options for planning, implementing and leading activities and events. The competition with other hearing students is stiff and the size of public schools makes developing leadership skills difficult, if not impossible. Deaf teenagers need a place to practice leadership and Deaf ministries should make this a priority. Mission opportunities provide active participation in the learning process and development of important planning and implementation skills. The Christian faith teaches leadership in its proper perspective; one must first become a servant as Christ served the Apostles.[93] This is an important perspective that is missed in most of the secular leadership training programs.

It will be an exciting day when Deaf teenagers have dozens of opportunities each year for mission trips domestically and abroad. It is inspiring to envision the new level of Deaf leadership that will evolve from these experiences within this next generation; a generation committed to reaching the world for Christ. As a minister involved in the beginning of the Third Wave of Deaf ministry, I predict that Deaf teenagers involved in *missions* will become one of the most identifiable characteristics of this era. There has already been some movement in this direction but we have barely begun. If you are a believer in our Lord, I ask for your prayers for this revival to become mission-minded and full of opportunity for young Deaf people to bring light to the world through their love and service.

Outreach and relational ministry—Relational ministry is the only viable means of reaching this next generation of Deaf children and youth with the gospel of Jesus Christ. There are three basic parts of programming to this generation: *outreach, discipleship,* and *missions.* Outreach is how we reach the scattered population of unchurched Deaf young people. Make your activities fun and *on-the-edge*; teenagers want to have fun! God has begun a revival in our land to reach the Deaf of the Diaspora and it is a spiritual and relational experience.

Third Wave ministries must be able to relate to young people who are unchurched in every sense of the word. They will likely have dirty minds, hands, and habits. The love of the leaders must be stronger than the pain of the youth. Youth ministry leaders must have great compassion and tolerance for confused and hurting individuals without compromising the gospel of Jesus Christ. Jesus reached out to the leper, the prostitute, the drunk, the greedy tax collector, the demon possessed and other sinners. Jesus said, *"It is not the healthy who need a doctor, but the sick."*[94] He also railed against the self-righteous, religious leaders who made these very people feel lowly and despised. Jesus accepts you wherever you are, but He doesn't leave you there; he takes your hand and leads you out of sin. We must have ministries that do likewise.

There was a day when the greatest challenge of Deaf ministry was finding enough leaders to supervise the teenagers. There was a day when the primary issue was accessibility; if you built it, they would come. We are reaching out to an almost completely secular population. They have been excluded from many of the most fundamental concepts of the Christian faith. Jesus tells us a parable in Luke 14 about the Great Banquet and our need to fill the room with His people. *"Then the master told his servant, 'Go out to the roads and country lanes and make them come in, so that my house will be full.'"* (verse 23, NIV) The Master recognizes that this group of people may include folks who do not fit into a traditional religious setting but he invites them anyway. In fact, Jesus sends us out to find them. This is outreach.

Relational ministry has also been described as *friendship evangelism*. Author Keith Miller coined a beautiful description of the gospel when he claimed *the Kingdom of God is the kingdom of right relationships*. Faithfulness to the gospel brings us into peace with God, others, and ourselves. Some quote the JOY acronym that stands for *Jesus, Others, Yourself*, in that order for a meaningful, fulfilling life. The greatest commandments, as Jesus told us, are *"Love the Lord your God with all your heart and with all your soul and with all your strength and with all your mind; and love your neighbor as yourself."* (Luke 10:27) The same three components appear in this Scripture; we must learn to *love God, our neighbor,* and *ourselves*. Sometimes, the most difficult challenge for a teenager is learning to love him or herself. This is why Christian adult leaders are so vital in expressing God's love to teenagers who struggle with issues of identity and belonging.

Youth For Christ has developed an evangelism-training program called *Three Story Evangelism* written by Bill Muir. It describes the interaction of three stories: your story, my story and God's story. First, I listen intently to your story and find ways it is similar to my story; then, I share my story and how I have been influenced by God's story. Finally, I share God's story and how it may also become part of your story. This may be an oversimplification of the process, but it is basic relational evangelism and a way for sharing the gospel naturally and effectively.

Effective Third Wave ministry has Biblical foundations (First Wave), is tuned-in to the culture environment of the Deaf person (Second Wave) yet focuses primarily on the one-to-one relationship that provides friendship, fun, support, and honesty about the importance of right relationships with self, others, and God. It is essentially earning the right to share the gospel with another person through unconditional love for that person.

Technology, DraMuSign, Deaf-Music, Basic Gospel—Technology has created an amazing ability for people to connect, and this new generation fully expects to be included in the benefits of a high tech society. They enjoy many of the same things that their hearing peers like including first-run movies, DVDs, dances, hip-hop music (or whatever is loud and popular at the time), televised sports, computer games, computers in general, and the Internet. Through high-speed Internet connections, Deaf people may carry on real-time, face-to-face conversations in ASL with computer video cameras. They may chat with their friends throughout the day with two-way pagers and wireless technology. Young Deaf people have a strong sense of connection through Instant Messaging with other Deaf people scattered across the country. There is virtually no dependency on hearing people for making phone calls. Telephone calls may now be made through the computer, either by text or through a Video Relay Service where the Deaf person signs to the operator who voices the telephone call and signs back the response.

This has given rise to what I jokingly refer to as the DFS—Deaf Fatigue Syndrome; young Deaf people staying awake all night chatting via computer and then being exhausted at work or school the next day. I also know some Deaf high school students whose grades are dropping dramatically as they spend most of the school day engaged in Instant Message conversations. With each new advancement in technology, there is a learning curve of how to appropriately use technology while avoiding the downside and dangers.

At the same time, technology does not replace the touch of a friend during a time of crisis or provide someone to hang out with at the shopping mall. The food court at the local mall has essentially replaced the Deaf club (and the church) for this generation. The Christian faith has been so obliterated from the lives of young Deaf people, either by neglect or intention of those around them, that that they may conclude there is little possibility of knowing and being known by God. Imagine living in a world without awareness of the One who created us and loves us. There is a deep yearning in the hearts of all young people for a belief that life matters, and what matters most is being part of something greater than oneself. The hope of the Deaf community is in those who are now children and youth who are part of a New Culture of Deafness.

Third Wave ministries must use the tried and true traditions of games, activities and social times but it is important to be intentional in creative programming. It is tempting to just toss out some snacks and let the young people chat. This is a huge mistake. Nature abhors a vacuum and so do young people. If you do not have a plan, they will develop their own plan and it may not be one of which you approve. Be intentional in preparing for active participation. Make the time productive. We do not have the luxury of just creating a junior Deaf club. We have so little time with young people now that programming should include socialization activities as well as drama, music (loud and with lots of bass),

DraMuSign (a phrase coined by Chad Entinger that combines drama, music and sign language), and a clear basic presentation of the gospel message from the New Testament focused on Jesus Christ.

As part of the discipleship program, particularly in church-based ministries, Chronological Bible Storying (CBS) is an excellent means of communicating the Bible to the Deaf community. It uses repetition and drama and breaks the Bible stories down into a sequential flow of information. The young people themselves act out the Jesus-stories; the individuals become part of the Scriptural narratives. This is not a new concept in Deaf ministry but an important tradition to keep alive. There must be a visual presentation of the information in a way that involves the Deaf person. You cannot just plug Deaf teenagers into hearing groups and expect them to learn in the same way as their hearing peers. Even with a skilled interpreter, it falls short of making sense in the Deaf-Mind. Active participation is a hallmark of effective Deaf ministry.

It is important to focus on the uncluttered basics of the gospel with this generation of Deaf young people. Personally, I prefer the uncluttered gospel, period; but here I am referring to the importance of *sequence, simplicity,* and *sincerity.* Do not hopscotch around the Bible with a devotional story here and inspirational thought there. This makes sense to people who have a foundational understanding of the flow of Biblical history, but most Deaf teenagers have no knowledge base of the Bible. It is difficult to make sense out of these seemingly disconnected messages and stories.

Jesus Christ is the *"visible image of the invisible God"* (Colossians 1:15, NLT) and is our best and clearest picture of God. Present the life of Christ in the order that it occurred. Focus on one point at a time. This creates a thirst for knowledge about this fascinating person Jesus, in the minds and hearts of the teenagers. Do not toss in a story about Noah and the Ark and then a devotional about King David. The average young person (Deaf *and* hearing) who did not grow up in the church will come away with a vague understanding that David rode on Noah's boat over the Red Sea to visit Jesus! Provide uncluttered, systematic presentation of information that reduces confusion. Small group Bible studies or one-to-one conversations are the place for exploring deeper theological issues. Jesus always seemed to disciple people either individually or as part of a small group interaction. When Jesus addressed the large group, it was always a clear, concise sharing of profound yet understandable truths.

Inclusion and unique programming (both)—Deaf teenagers are both Deaf and they are teenagers. Most are also being raised in a hearing world. Do not ignore their needs for participating with large groups of hearing teenagers for high-energy, exciting activities. Also, remember their need as Deaf individuals for participating in programming that is specifically designed for them.

Some of the mainstreamed teenagers who are more disconnected from the Deaf community may feel more comfortable in a setting with both hearing and Deaf teenagers. It gives them a safety net in case they feel rejected by other Deaf teenagers. What they usually find (if the ministry is healthy) is an almost instant and overwhelming connection with the other Deaf teenagers and a sense of belonging. They may experience this emotional connection in an event with a thousand hearing teens and twenty Deaf teens.

Effective Deaf ministry with young people involves *"fun, friendship, fellowship, and faith."*[95] Fun and friendship can happen in the hearing world. Fellowship and faith are best developed in a uniquely Deaf setting. Discipleship is most effective in a unique programming setting where Deaf teenagers process the information in a Deaf cultural model with sign language and with pacing that fits Deaf learning styles and preferences. Camps and mission trips may be in either inclusive or exclusive settings as long as there is an identifiable Deaf group where the young person is able to process the experience. This means that effective Third Wave ministries will occasionally participate in both interpreted hearing settings and consistently provide separate Deaf-Focused settings. The key is to be intentional. Your Deaf teenagers are the priority and do only what makes sense for them. Join in with the large group of hearing teens when there is a great opportunity for fun and new friendships. Have separate events for deeper spiritual and emotional interactions.

One caveat is to remember that Deaf teenagers (especially those who are mainstreamed) experience consistent exclusion in the hearing world due to the language and cultural barriers. They desperately need a place that is uniquely theirs where relationships are fully accessible. Deaf ministry with teenagers should not include hearing teens unless it is a clear benefit to individual Deaf teens. Whenever hearing teens are in the mix, the tendency is for ministries to lose focus on the Deaf teens. By the end of the event, the hearing and Deaf teens are standing around chatting, separately. Hearing teens have hundreds of opportunities to participate in youth programs. Deaf teens have very few that are completely for them and this Deaf event should never be sacrificed for the comfort of the hearing teens. Anyone who has been involved with Deaf ministry knows of the many requests from hearing people who are interested in learning sign language and want to attend your activities. Mixing hearing people with other agendas into the mix is a slippery slope and generally should be avoided. Young Deaf people rarely experience events that are completely designed for them; treasure this experience as your number one priority for them and guard it diligently.

Equal access to the Gospel—In the previous two chapters, the contrast between the views of the First and Second Waves with regards to the identity of Deaf people within ministry settings was described as the contrast between "We are all God's children" (*Deaf people need barriers removed through interpreters and sign language*) and "Deaf Identity and Rights" (*We are uniquely Deaf and therefore have a separate experience of faith from hearing people*). Third Wave ministries will take a third road that recognizes both the distinctiveness of being Deaf and the similarity of experiences in life shared with the hearing majority. "Equal access to the gospel" translates into *I am just like any other person who has the right to experience God in a personal way that makes sense to me as a Deaf individual.*

Although the Deaf person's experience with God is uniquely Deaf, it is also unified with other sincere Christians. A Deaf Christian and a hearing Christian have more in common with each other than either does with unbelievers of their same cultures. Christ unites us as His followers. The old saying holds true: *the ground is level at the foot of the cross.* Though we experience life differently, our fundamental spiritual, emotional, and relational needs are the same.

There are a number of ways that Deaf individuals will find equal access during this time of revival. One is through Deaf churches that are experiencing a renewed energy. Another way is through retreats specifically designed for Deaf men or women to gather, share and grow. The ASL Bible and Daily Devotionals for the Deaf, on-line in ASL and in written form are all part of equal access. The same eternal gospel is experienced across the ages, languages, and cultures.

A vital way Deaf Christians are finding equal access to the gospel is through changes in the educational opportunities for personal growth and training, largely brought about by technology. For example, The Deaf Institute of Theology at Concordia Seminary in St. Louis, Missouri was established in 1999 for training Lutheran leaders in the church as well as Deaf Lutheran pastors. Although there had been a Deaf ministry track in the seminary for a number of years, this program shows the transition that is occurring between the First to the Second and into the Third Wave of Deaf ministry. It is a program specifically designed for distance learning and finding ways to train the scattered population of Deaf individuals in ministry.

In the spring of 1998, a coalition of leaders from seventeen Deaf ministries met to discuss the challenges facing Deaf ministry. They were led by Rev. Ray Berry and Dr. Sharon Berry of Christian Deaf Fellowship in Birmingham, Alabama. The leaders were from different organizations and denominations who shared basic principles: a commitment to God's Word, the need for salvation through Jesus Christ, the importance of Deaf leadership, respect for differences in traditions and doctrinal perspectives. What emerged is the Deaf Evangelical Agencies in Fellowship for Christ (D.E.A.F. for Christ).

One major need that all agreed upon was training for Deaf people involved in ministry. Out of their efforts grew the interdenominational distance-learning program, Christian Deaf Virtual University. Courses are offered on-line in ASL through live video streaming. The distance-learning program has partnered with Gardner-Webb University in North Carolina to offer college-level courses for credit in Deaf ministry. The barriers of the past in theological training were being removed through technology. This allows for equal access to opportunities for spiritual maturity and training for ministry. D.E.A.F for Christ is an excellent example of a visionary effort to bring together evangelical ministries to find new ways to reach the scattered population of Deaf people with the gospel message. It is an example of a Third Wave adaptation to the needs of the new century.[96]

ASL with acceptance of other communication styles—At a recent meeting about Deaf ministry, three Deaf men were in a conversation. The Deaf man in his forties kept looking to a Deaf man in his thirties to interpret what a Deaf man in his twenties was signing. All three were Deaf; all three were signing in ASL but the older and the younger men could not understand each other. There was a communication and generational barrier between these two Deaf individuals separated by little more than one decade.

This reflects the radical changes that had occurred in the Deaf community during the twelve years that separated the older and younger Deaf men's ages both literally and symbolically. The Deaf man in his forties became a Christian under First Wave leadership, was involved as a volunteer during the Second Wave and has basically been unable to transition to Third Wave ministry. The younger Deaf man is an archetype of the next generation. He signs ASL, tends to think in English, loves to communicate through technology and the written word, and moves relatively easily in both the hearing and Deaf worlds. The Deaf man in his thirties provided the link. This was really more of a generation gap than a lack of communication skills.

Third Wave ministries must adapt to the communication needs of the individual. A Deaf/Oral person also needs to understand the gospel and may be limited due to the inability to sign. Many Deaf/Oral people experience exclusion in the hearing world yet cannot find acceptance in the Deaf-World. This must change. We must make every possible accommodation to connect all Deaf people with their Creator regardless of their preferred style of communication. This is part of accepting people as they are and loving them into the Kingdom of God.

In reality, Deaf individuals who do not sign will begin to learn sign language when they become involved with a caring community of Deaf people whose first language is signing. It is so incredibly freeing to be able to express oneself with moving hands, body posture, expressions, and gestures. This may become the result of effective Deaf ministry but it is not the goal. Christ calls us to share with the world his message of hope and reflect it in our love for each other. Recently, a Deaf teenager who knew virtually no sign language attended a weekly small group Bible study for the first time. She was quite uncomfortable when she first arrived. One of the young, Deaf female leaders was a woman who also grew up Deaf-Oral. This leader reached out to this young lady and immediately made a connection because of their common background. The leader began by only speaking without sign language until the teenager's comfort level rose and then began adding signs while she spoke. The leader's response was loving, non-judgmental, intentional, and relational.

Another change that needs to occur in our thinking with regards to ministry in the 21st Century is to cease use of the "little d" and "big D" when referring to members of this community. Who decides whether someone is in or out? Does the person himself/herself have a say? Everyone would agree that there are large numbers of people who cannot hear who do not connect with anything Deaf; however, these people will likely prefer the term "hearing impaired" because this is how they see themselves. This is their right. Whenever Christians use the term "d/Deaf" to define others, it creates a sense of insiders and outsiders. How does this mesh with the Christian faith? Is there such a thing as "s/Sinners" based on the severity of our sin? No. Did Jesus refer to the tax-gathers, sinners, and Pharisees as "j/Jews"? No. Do we refer to our church members as "c/Christians" based on who is *really* a Christian? Jesus put aside labels and welcomed people into the family of God as His followers. We are to do likewise.

Many times, people who sign in American Sign Language have a difficult time communicating in signed English. People who think in English word order and structures may have little or no understanding of American Sign Language. Those who do not sign at all may be even more isolated when participating in a Deaf ministry event than in a hearing ministry. So, how does a Third Wave ministry bridge these gaps? The answer is in having a diverse group of leaders from a variety of backgrounds. No one is excluded. All are welcomed into the kingdom of God. ASL should be the primary mode of communication with tolerance for all other preferences and accommodations made.

Priority on personal relationships—The key characteristic of Third Wave ministries that makes everything else work is a priority on personal relationships. Working with teenagers can be intoxicating. Many adults find that they are much more popular than they ever were when they were in middle or high school. This is a cautionary note and another reason it is vital to minister as part of a team with accountability and support. A leader may begin to feel responsible for personal ministry with dozens of teenagers. A *messiah complex* is a fast track to ministerial burnout that ultimately hurts those with whom you minister.

Young people need stability and dependability in relationships. Leaders need to have their own emotional needs met in church and through relationships with other adults. A leader should have only one to three significant relationships with teenagers to be able to sustain those friendships. The leader should be friendly and connected with everyone in the group but in terms of really investing time in consistent ministry relationships, there are clear limits. A team of ten Christian adults can have a huge impact on the lives of twenty to thirty young people in a community using this model. Imagine the influence of two dozen strong Christian Deaf teenagers in your community as they learn to minister to their friends. Faith is much more *caught* than *taught*. You are modeling for them a balanced and faithful life. You are also showing them your commitment to be consistent and reliable in a world fraught with sudden and unexpected change. As described in the previous section on building a diverse and unified team of leaders, relational ministry requires a ministry team. Each person on the team is an important part of the relational, outreach ministry to Deaf teenagers. Effective Third Wave ministries will help each member of the team develop the necessary skills for fulfilling God's call in his or her life.

In the next section, specific suggestions are made regarding relational ministry with Deaf teenagers. One vital truth that merits repeating: relational ministry is not about being popular with Deaf teenagers. Relational ministry is showing Deaf teenagers how much God loves them by how much the leaders love them. We are ambassadors for God. We are messengers of a God who loves them and wants a personal relationship with them. Relational ministry is helping a Deaf teenager experience acceptance, connection, a sense of place, identity, and meaningful relationships. The focus should never become solely relational; there is a much more important goal. It is through caring friendships that Deaf teenagers understand the life-giving relationship through Jesus Christ that comes from knowing and responding to God's love.

Someone once said *every teenager in the world needs to know there is some caring adult who is just crazy about them!* Youth ministry is not a burden; it is an honor to share one's life with young people. God's revival in the Deaf community is beginning through the Deaf children and youth who are born during the last half of the Second Wave. They will become the leaders who reach the Deaf community with the gospel. They are the hope of the Christian faith within the Deaf community. Effective Third Wave ministry will help this next generation find the spiritual center of deafness and emerge as the cultural core for the future of Deaf-World. As described in Chapter 1, *the main bond that holds together a cultural group during Diaspora is a foundational belief in a God who will guide them; a God who keeps them united, even while scattered.* A great deal rests on our ability to adapt to the changing realities of Deaf-World.

Personal Narrative ─────────────────────────── Chad Entinger

When did you become a Christian? If we were to take a survey of the people reading this book, most would probably respond, *"When I was young."*

Surveys have been conducted to determine when people become Christians. By far, most Christians became so before turning age eighteen. This is not surprising. The family and church has and will always have the greatest impact on what children grow up to become and the faith that he or she holds.

One small church and family had a profound impact on Deaf and hard of hearing children who grew up in their community. One small church and family intensely focused on the children and youth, as part of family units yet with respect to deafness, in connecting them to Jesus. Among the people in this small town of 1,200 people were two deaf boys, Peter and Brian. This town existed in a rural area, forty-five minutes from a major metropolitan area. A small church of about eighty members hosted typical Sunday morning services with hymns and Sunday School classes.

This church made sacrifices so that Peter and Brian would have opportunities to connect with Jesus. The members of this church sacrificed their time. It sometimes took longer to communicate with Peter and Brian. They took extra time to gesture. Sometimes, writing with paper and pen or on a chalkboard was the best way to communicate. Sometimes the members would speak more slowly and clearly so that Peter and Brian could speech-read some of what they were trying to say. During Vacation Bible School weeks, the schedule would include game time. Extra time was taken so Peter and Brian would understand the rules of the game being played.

The members of this church sacrificed their experiences. The hearing members were accustomed to experiences of learning about Jesus through auditory means. Hearing people are accustomed to learning about Jesus through the radio, a preacher speaking on Sunday morning, a Sunday School teacher lecturing, audiotapes, music songs, etc. Deaf people don't learn with their ears, but rather with their eyes. This church realized this and made sacrifices to help Peter and Brian. Church members used visuals (charts, pictures, flannel-graphs, etc.) when teaching Peter and Brian about Jesus.

The members of this church sacrificed their first and most convenient language. Some in this church learned sign language. Peter's parents and Brian's parents learned sign language. Instead of instruction in English, the church supported Peter's father as he used sign language to teach the Bible to Peter and

Brian. It surely was much easier for Peter and Brian to learn about the Bible through sign language as opposed to spoken English. Some members learned sign phrases. One time, the pastor's wife asked Peter to teach his classmates how to sign a song. And the classmates learned to present the song in sign language instead of singing.

The members of this church sacrificed their finances. This church financially supported Peter's father when he attended a conference sponsored by Deaf Missions of Council Bluffs, Iowa. At this conference, Peter's father learned about exciting opportunities in deaf ministry and a variety of ways to help deaf people understand who Jesus is. This church gave Peter's father space in the church building to teach Sunday School and Vacation Bible School classes for Peter and Brian. They also financed needed visuals.

This church's intense focus on the deaf children in its own community produced eternal soul-saving results. Peter became a Christian at eight years old. As an adult today, he is still an active, serving Christian. He has brought other deaf people to Jesus. He actively leads a church for Deaf people. He teaches weekly classes for Deaf adults as well as classes for Deaf children and teenagers.

Before you move on to the next chapter, I want you to realize one thing. Peter is my middle name. I am the beneficiary of the kindness of others. I am personally grateful for the people who shared with me the most important story in history: the truth of Jesus Christ and God's desire for a relationship with me.

Discussion and Review

Waves THREE
Chapter 7—Third WAVE

Expressions

Talk with some Deaf teenagers; ask them to describe their experience as a young person. How different is it from the other hearing teenagers? How is it similar?

Challenge

Get a catalogue on technology that targets a Deaf audience. Make note of the independence that much of the technology brings to Deaf individuals. How do you think this might change the dynamics between Deaf people and their hearing peers? Where do barriers still exist?

What are the possible pros and cons of each of the defining traits of Third Wave ministries?

What are the key factors that changed in our culture that brought about the New Culture of Deafness? What key traits do the Third Wave ministries need to maintain for reaching this generation with the gospel?

Scripture

"Trust in the Lord with all your heart and lean not on your own understanding. In all your ways, acknowledge Him and He will make your paths straight." Proverbs 3:5-6

The Third Wave is a time of great hope and revival within the Deaf community. Even though many things changed, how does this Scripture affirm the hope that is found in God's love and presence? What are the dangers that might hinder this revival during the beginning of the 21st Century?

Application

How does this description of the Third Wave resonate with your own experience? What positive traits do we need to use in ministry during the 21st Century? How does this understanding affect your perspective on Deaf ministry?

How can we provide opportunities for Deaf teenagers during the Third Wave to mature into the leaders for the future of Christian ministry? What do you believe will be next following the Third Wave?

Vision IMPACT
Section III

"Where there is no vision, the people perish..." Proverbs 29:18

Deaf Time

At the inaugural Deaf Teen Ministry National Symposium in 2001, I closed our meeting together with the words, "It's Time." Repeating these words and tapping my watch, I expressed a deep sense of the beginning of a revival across our land. It was an awesome awareness of God's vision for reaching his people at this particular juncture. The time is now. It is Deaf time. It is the Deaf turn for a revival that redeems both individuals and a community for Christ. The impact of the national symposium on our lives was huge as God brought us together to experience Christian community from across the country and the denominational spectrum. We are God's people and we are called to work together for his purposes. We cannot delay. We cannot remain separate. The Evil One has kept us weak by keeping us divided. To become strong, we must be willing to come together. But we are no longer orphans in a storm. We are family. Together, we become the church, and the gates of hell cannot stand against us.

Vision. IMPACT.

By responding to God's vision of reaching Deaf teenagers with the gospel of Jesus Christ, we are able to enjoy being part of the impact of God's Spirit moving in this world. We may be riding the Third Wave but God is the creator of ALL the waves throughout history. He was reaching the Deaf community long before any of us were alive and He will continue long after we are gone. Now, at this particular point in time, we must respond to the changes in our world with wisdom and intention. We must find new ways to share an old story to a new generation. We are the Body of Christ; He has called us and the time is now.

It is Deaf time.

God has created each person beautiful and perfect in His eyes regardless of our perceived differences. Defining oneself by who one is not (i.e. cannot hear) is sad and borders on insulting the Creator. I cannot fly. Does this make me "wing-impaired?" No. I am created in the image of God as a creature that walks instead of flaps. Are birds "fin-impaired" because they do not swim? How absurd! Are women "gender-impaired?" Not on your life! One should never be defined by what cannot be done. We are as God has made us.

The angels celebrated every birth (both physically and spiritually) with a boisterous cheer! Angel hands fly joyfully when that person is born Deaf; whether one can hear sound or not is not a significant issue. Those angels celebrate when that same Deaf person comes into a personal relationship with God. They shake their hands in Deaf-Applause and praise God in the language of the Deaf person. The heavenly hosts are omni-linguistic. Jesus said, *"In the same way God's angels are happy when even one person turns to Him."* (Luke 15:10, CEV)

It is time for a new vision for reconnecting the Deaf community with the gospel of Jesus Christ. We cannot turn the clock back to an earlier day when most

Deaf gathered around the schools for the Deaf; they are a scattered people. With God's help, we can create a new way for Christian Deaf, hard of hearing and hearing adults to invest their lives into the lives of Deaf teenagers. It is a new day! The time is now.

The teenage years are the most important ones for making lifelong (and eternal) decisions. A person with an idyllic childhood may destroy his or her life by making bad choices during the teen years. A person with a horrid childhood may come into a personal relationship with God and flourish. After high school, relatively few people accept Christ. It is those who are teenagers now who will reach the next generation of Deaf young adults with the gospel. The spiritual hope of the Deaf community lies with those who are now children and youth.

Hearing teenagers have enjoyed excellent quality youth programs for many years. In the past, Deaf teenagers had some opportunities. Now, there are few, painfully few, ministries specifically for Deaf and hard of hearing teenagers. God has spoken; God has signed.

It is Deaf time.

"By this all will know that you are My disciples…if you have love for one another." (John 13:35, NKJV). It is love that changes the heart of the lonely, the mind of the confused, the strength of the weary, the soul of the isolated; it is love that defends the faith and teaches it to a new generation. God calls us as a community to reembrace the spiritual legacy that once was integral to Deaf-World. God is pursuing the Deaf individual and no longer will being Deaf become a barrier to understanding the greatest gift given to humanity.

It is Deaf time.

Now, finish, now.

The time is now; we cannot delay.

Deaf time, now.

Sections One and Two of this book (Deaf DIASPORA and Waves THREE) provide a conceptual framework for Deaf ministry during the 21st Century. Although it is still from a distinctively Christian perspective, both sections are written with a general audience in mind. For those who are primarily interested in the theoretical aspects of the book, sections one and two are designed to give a structural framework for making sense of the radical changes that have occurred in Deaf-World.

Section Three—Vision IMPACT—brings a shift in writing style and focus. It contains more information that applies specifically to individuals or groups interested in Christian outreach to Deaf and hard of hearing teenagers. Vision IMPACT applies to those with a passion for practical ministry with Deaf teenagers and particularly interested in Deaf Teen Quest (DTQuest). Vision IMPACT helps those who are interested in the application of these theories and observations contained in the first two sections of the book in the form of Christian ministry with this new generation of Deaf teenagers.

Chapter 8—Ministry with Teenagers

A Deaf teenager belongs to at least three cultural groups: Deaf, Youth, and Family.

Describe your average teenager.

Indiscernible slang...wild clothing...radical thoughts...rebellious attitudes...takes unnecessary risks...passion for fun...interest in sex...obsession on "fitting in"...flirtatious behavior...attraction to thrills...pushing of limits...moody...concerns about future...uncertainty about self...moments of amazing maturity...hot and cold friendships...stressed with academics...insights about life...fear of failure...questions about God...It is an exhausting time for the adolescent and all those around them!

The clothing styles may change with the passing of the years but the pressure to wear the right styles is constant. Popular hair styles may be short, long, curly, bleached, braided or black but the pressuring awareness of *"what's cool"* and *"what's not"* is common for all generations of adolescents. The acceptable exclamation may change from *"cool"* to *"groovy"* to *"bad"* to *"awesome"* to *"phat"* to *"hot"* and back to *"cool"* but the tendency of teenagers is to compress a myriad of emotions in a single exclamation is eternal! This common experience is part of what defines a cultural group. In this case, we are referring to the youth culture; those years between thirteen and nineteen (although some try to extend this into the twenties) which are identified as *adolescence*.

Cultures of a Deaf Teenager

There are three foundational cultures of the Deaf teenager: youth, family (including ethnicity), and Deaf. Other sub-cultures influence the Deaf teenager based on personal preferences and involvement. Effective ministry recognizes the cultural distinctiveness of a Deaf adolescent and responds to the individual needs of the teenager as influenced by this multi-cultural environment.

Adolescents are part of a general cultural group (youth culture) simply because of their ages. Teenagers share in a developmental process common with young people throughout history and around the world. There is a teenage culture (although diverse in nature) based on the common experience of living in transition from childhood to adulthood. There are individual exceptions—usually due to unusual circumstances such as war, famine, or family crisis—but in essence, teenagers around the world, including those who are Deaf, experience similar challenges.

Young people are part of the culture of their families and communities. Consider the diversity of teenagers in our country; they come from every background imaginable. Some teenagers are from Hispanic, Asian, African-American or other ethnic communities, while others are Caucasian and part of some socio-economic class within the majority population. Some navigate in large metropolitan areas while their peers dwell in the back roads of the country. Some live and play in government-subsidized housing while others reside in suburban mansions and belong to the Country Club. Some travel the world with their families while others never leave the region of their birth. Some families never expect anyone to graduate from high school while others will settle for nothing less than advanced degrees from elite colleges. Generally, teenagers reflect the values of their families and communities.

Deaf teenagers are members of this distinct cultural group that has undergone radical redefinition due to the Deaf Diaspora. Many Deaf teenagers, particularly those who are hard of hearing, sense a commonality with Deaf-World but may feel disconnected with the experience of those who are completely Deaf. Deaf-World offers barrier-free communication and cultural understanding. Once a Deaf or hard of hearing person has made this emotional and social connection, deafness becomes a dramatic part of one's sense of self, arguably the defining cultural identity for the individual. Being Deaf becomes woven into ones' identity and connection with others.

Consider all the other sub-cultural groups a Deaf teenager may choose to join. There are cultures connected with groups such as the drama club, athletics, Jr. ROTC, National Honor Society, Future Business Leaders of America and the Fellowship of Christian Athletes. Other sub-cultures such as gangs, cults, and alternative lifestyles can negatively impact a teen's life as they strive for identity. The media and Internet become sources for thousands of differing and conflicting cultural messages. It is no wonder that teenagers seem so emotional; it can be overwhelming to make sense out of all these cultural influences. This does not even include the rapid physical changes and intense hormonal influences in the lives of teenagers.

One is undeniably influenced by each of the cultural groups to which he or she belongs. What happens when these diverse cultures of a Deaf teenager clash?

What if the culture of the family conflicts with the expectations of the Deaf-World? A Deaf teenager is part of *all* the cultures that give form to his or her identity. One key to emotional stability is to assimilate these disparate influences into a singular sense of self. No one exists in a vacuum; we are all inheritors of our heritage. We are the legacy of those who have gone before us.

Throughout adolescence, teens tend to identify less with parents and more with their peer group and other adults. This is one of the reasons having positive, Christian adult role models and friends are so critical during these years. It is important for ministries to work along with the family to provide a sense of stability and support for teens who are making this transition from childhood to adulthood.

Teenagers need caring adults who can help them make it through this challenging experience of *growing up*. A critical goal of adolescence is to successfully integrate all of these conflicting cultural experiences into some form of a healthy identity. The age-old question of *"Who am I?"* becomes *"THIS is who I am,"* and for the Christian, *"This is who GOD has created me to be."*

Spiritual health is an important aspect of developing ones' personal identity; believing that *I am created in the image of God and therefore my life has value.* Many Christians define this as receiving *abundant life* in Christ.[97] Naturally, counseling or medication may be an important part of a person's mental health, but this fundamental sense of being created in the image of God, for His purposes, is the bedrock of emotional stability. It is important to focus on these basic truths: there is a God who created us, we are a beautiful creation, our sin has separated us from God yet He desperately wants a personal relationship with each of us. God has provided a way for this reconnection to occur through the life, death and resurrection of Jesus Christ. This understanding helps develop a sense of, *If God can love me that much; then my life must certainly have worth.*

Developmental Tasks of Adolescents

Erik Erikson, a neo-Freudian psychoanalyst, was a significant figure in the field of Developmental Psychology. He describes eight stages in life through which people transition as they age.[98] Each stage presents particular challenges for the individual called *developmental tasks.* If one does not successfully pass through one developmental stage, he or she is unable to succeed in future stages. Through therapy, one is able to address the unfulfilled needs at an earlier stage and then get back on track towards emotional stability and maturity. The positive outcomes of each stage are, in order…trust, autonomy, initiative, industry, identity, intimacy, generativity (willingness to help the next generation), and ego-integrity (confidence in having lived a fulfilling life).

A cursory description is given of three of the developmental stages described by Erikson that seem most directly to affect teenagers. The first developmental stage in a person's life begins immediately after birth and is a question of **Trust versus Mistrust**. A newborn learns that his or her environment is either *trustworthy* or *not trustworthy*. If an infant is nourished and nurtured—consistently experiences a caring environment—he or she will have a fundamental trust of the surrounding world. If not, he or she will subconsciously believe the world is not a trusting place and this will affect all his or her relationships. This is one of the reasons why building *trust* is a high priority of working with teenagers. Teenagers need to experience dependability in others to understand the reliability of God's love. If the teenager has not experienced the world as a trustworthy place, this is easily transferred to distrust of God's goodness and power.

There are a three other developmental stages before the teenage years but the primary challenge of adolescence, according to this theory, is the developmental task of **Identity versus Role Confusion**. This is a time of discerning *self* as a distinct and independent being. This is the experience of questioning, *"Who Am I? Am I the person my parents, teachers, and friends have told me I am or am I someone else?"* Teenagers are in the process of making critical, lifelong decisions about their identity. These years are *so* critical in the development of healthy self-esteem and identity. If the teenager is successful in progressing through the teen years with a positive sense of identity, he or she will have a fundamental belief in the goodness of life. Positive self-esteem produces healthier relationships, greater happiness, and better overall success in life.

Part of this developmental task for a teenager is the need to learn to relate adequately to *persons* of the same gender and *a* person of the opposite gender. There is the need for confidence in being *one of the guys (or gals)*. There is a need for expressing oneself and being unique, yet fitting in with the crowd. At the same time, it is a time to learn relationship skills with *a* person of the opposite sex.[99] An important part of developing meaningful boyfriend/girlfriend relationships is learning to set boundaries as an expression of respect and sharing in the relationship. Adolescence is a time of learning to love and be loved; and overcoming the challenges of jealousy, emotional obsession, perceived and real oppression, and the danger of losing one's identity in another person.

The developmental task that follows adolescence (during young adulthood) is **Intimacy versus Isolation**. Without a sense of identity, young adults cannot truly experience intimacy. Intimacy is *not* a code word for sex. Intimacy means being known and loved for who you are. It involves having developed a sense of self and comfortably sharing oneself with another. Intimacy between friends, and within marriages, is built upon all these earlier stages, beginning with trust.

When families lack adequate signing skills, these developmental tasks become more difficult for Deaf children. It is not *deafness* that makes these stages more challenging; it is the *absence of effective communication* by those around the Deaf individual. In other words, a Deaf person who grows up in a signing environment can successfully pass through each stage, with the same rate of success as a hearing person. The reality is that most Deaf children are growing up in non-signing environments, particularly during the Deaf Diaspora, and therefore these developmental stages may become particularly challenging. Part of an effective ministry will be sensitive to the emotional needs of teenagers to build trust, autonomy, initiative, industry, and identity. The end result will be people who, as adults, will have a greater likelihood of enjoying intimacy, generativity, and ego-integrity.

"Fun, Friendship, Fellowship, Faith"

There are four words that describe the basic social, emotional, and spiritual needs of teenagers: *fun, friendship, fellowship, faith*.[100] One must begin with the priorities of a teenager; they want to be *happy*, which means, having *friends* and *fun*. As adults, we recognize they also have more profound needs for a place to express their deepest emotional feelings without communication barriers (fellowship) and a fundamental understanding of their place in the cosmos as a beautiful creation in the image of God (faith). These are foundational building blocks for an abundant life.

Fun

Jim Rayburn, founder of the Young Life ministry says it best when it comes to fun in ministry, *"It is a sin to bore a kid with the gospel."*[101] Kids need to have fun. To reach Deaf and hard of hearing teenagers with the gospel, we must recognize their needs as teenagers. Teenagers have a strong desire to gather, have fun, and socialize. They need to take risks, be *wild and crazy* and burn off some energy. They need to be surprised and to laugh. They need to be children who can be silly and tease each other. Some religious groups tend to make the gospel (Good News) painfully boring and judgmental. Jesus proclaimed during his opening sermon when he announced that he was the promised Messiah *"The Spirit of the Lord is on me, because he has anointed me to preach good news to the poor. He has sent me to proclaim freedom for the prisoners and recovery of sight for the blind, to release the oppressed, to proclaim the year of the Lord's favor."* (Luke 4:18-19, NIV). Another time, Jesus explained, *"I came so they might have life, a great full life."* (John 10:10, NLV). It is a *blast* to follow Jesus. Sure, it is tough and there will be dark days of the soul but Jesus exploded onto the scene with a chorus of angels cheering Him and praising God for the new day in this world of sin. Keep it fun. God is the author of light, hope and laughter.

Friendship

We all want to be liked; we want to have friends. The theme from the television show *Cheers* expresses this need. *"Sometimes you want to go where everybody knows your name and they're always glad you came. You wanna be where you can see, our troubles are all the same. You wanna be where everybody knows your name."[102]* It is a sad commentary that the world tends to associate friendship more with the environment of a pub than at a gathering of Christians. Probably even more important than fun is to create a place of *friendship*. Friendship is particularly important during the teen years. Creating a positive peer group helps a teenager develop important social skills and self-esteem. More mature teenagers who are already Christians are vital; peer relationships are more important to a teenager than anything and Christian teenagers can have a profound effect on younger and newer members of the group. Young people need friendships with older role models as well. Christian adults provide helpful guidance and influence in the lives of young people through meaningful friendships.

Fellowship

In the Bible, the word for *fellowship* in the original Greek is *koinonia*. It is through Jesus that we learn how to love God, others and self. Koinonia is the experience of authentic, loving relationships with people who really know us. It is closely associated with the concept of the Body of Christ. The opposite of koinonia is isolation that is expressed in a number of self-destructive ways; at its core is the unfulfilled need *to know and be known*. As relational ministry moves more deeply into the emotional and spiritual needs of teenagers, *fellowship* is where the needs for clear communication in ASL become more critical. We must recognize the need of Deaf teenagers to make sense out of the gospel in their own language with sensitivity to the Deaf thought-processes. To experience this level of fellowship, it becomes important for Deaf teenagers to be able to express themselves freely in a language and culture that makes sense. By reducing communication barriers, teens can share their feelings and thoughts more deeply and experience the healing that comes with true fellowship.

Faith

In addition to meeting the needs of *fun, friendship* and *fellowship*, there is a deeper need in Deaf teenagers to experience and commit to faith in God. To develop fully devoted followers of Jesus Christ, we must recognize the unique needs and experiences of those who are deaf. To make sense of God's love, they must understand the information without muddle or barrier. The most direct and uncluttered way is directly into the Deaf-Mind through ASL. This removes any sense of the cultural and communication hindrances that may make one feel like a second-class citizen in the Kingdom of God. The development of faith must be focused primarily on helping Deaf young people develop a direct, personal relationship with Jesus Christ. *"He is the image of the invisible God, the first-born over all creation."* (Colossians 1:15, NIV) Growth as a Christian follows through Bible study, prayer, fellowship, and mentoring from older Christians.

We want them to experience this relationship, *develop a love for Scripture as authority in their life,* and have *opportunities to serve, minister, and lead.* An important aspect of personal faith in Christ is understanding the gospel message in the way that makes sense to you as an individual. A visual presentation of the gospel is vital to help young Deaf people grasp abstract concepts and make informed decisions about following Christ and understanding the Biblical message. We need to recognize the uniqueness of Deaf thought-processes and respect the cultural preferences of this young person.

This chart describes the unique dynamics of the movement into understanding about the Christian faith as a Deaf young person. The first two areas (fun and friendship) can occur in the hearing world. Fun and friendship are so vital simply because they are teenagers. The second two (fellowship—*deep friendship*—and faith) must be processed cognitively and experientially as a Deaf person. They are Deaf and process information differently from their hearing peers. Sharing on a deeper level requires fluency in sign language. When trying to fully understanding the abstract concepts inherent to the Christian faith (i.e. grace, forgiveness, atonement, holiness), one has moved almost totally into the Deaf thought processes. Making sense of the gospel and maturing in faith requires moving past any communication and cultural barriers. This barrier-free communication is how Deaf youth are able to fully experience *koinonia* (fellowship) and grasp a profound understanding and experience of faith in Christ.

It may be easy to brush past this section without recognizing the importance of this fundamental concept. This concept is seminal in programming for Deaf teen ministry during the Third Wave. Effective Deaf ministries will intentionally include opportunities for Deaf and hard of hearing teenagers to experience ministry in all four areas: *fun, friendship, fellowship, faith*.

A Deaf Teenager's needs...

...as a TEENAGER

...as a DEAF person

Fun   Friendship   Fellowship   Faith

Relational Evangelism

Joseph Bayly, a journalist who became the director of InterVarsity Press in 1951, penned a parable *The Gospel Blimp*. It tells of a group of Christians who want to evangelize their neighbors so they hatch a plan for dropping evangelical tracts on them from a blimp. It was a satirical look at evangelism without relationship and the importance of every Christian reaching out relationally instead of just leaving that task to the ordained leadership. Third Wave ministry in the Deaf-World has to recognize the unique experience of deafness for each individual and the diversity of young people with whom God has called us to minister. We cannot drop tracts on them or even depend on a single messenger to explain the gospel to them. We must understand people holistically, individually, and as part of a larger common experience of being Deaf in a hearing world.

There is so much we can learn from the hearing world that applies to ministry during the Deaf Diaspora. There are a number of para-church organizations reaching out to hearing teenagers who are scattered. The two that provide the greatest insight for outreach and relational ministry are *Youth For Christ* and *Young Life*. Any effective Third Wave ministry will make it a priority to develop a collegial relationship with the leaders of these two organizations and other similar ministries. There are many resources and insights that come from sharing and cooperation.

Youth For Christ (YFC) came into existence during the 1940s as a result of large youth rallies across the country. In 1945, a group of pastors organized the official ministry under the name *Youth For Christ* and hired a young Billy Graham as their first full-time staff member. During the 1950s, there was a focusing of the ministry specifically on teenagers, but it was still largely for young people who were already Christians. The primary programs during the 1950s were *Bible Clubs* for learning and memorizing Scripture. During the 1960s, in response to all the changes occurring in society, YFC sharpened their outreach to non-church young people under the program name of *Campus Life*. Today, YFC has a number of niche ministries and a relatively decentralized organizational structure. This means that local areas have much autonomy for responding to the ministry needs in their own communities. Although it began in the mid-west, the national headquarter is now in Englewood, Colorado. They are over 200 ministry areas in the United States and the ministry exists in over 100 countries around the world.[103]

Young Life began in 1941 under the leadership of a Presbyterian youth minister in Texas named Jim Rayburn. The consistent, primary thrust of *Young Life* is outreach and relational ministry to high school students through a trained, supervised team of caring Christian adults. For a number of years, *Young Life* has ministered in urban areas with adaptations made with sensitivity to African-American culture. More recently, *Young Life* has begun moving into more niche ministry for identifiable people groups with unique needs such as the *Young Lives* ministry to teenage mothers and the *Capernaum Ministry* for people with disabilities. They describe their relational ministry context with *"Young Life leaders model trust, respect and responsibility to their young friends, and they do it within a meaningful context, within the context of a teenager's world."*[104] Their national headquarters is in Colorado Springs, Colorado and they are active in every state and over 45 countries around the world. One of their strongest assets is the incredible quality of programming at their summer camps with twenty-four different properties across North America with facilities on the level of vacation resorts.

Two other important resources to note are the *National Network of Youth Ministries* and *Youth Specialties*. Headquartered in San Diego, California, the National Network of Youth Ministries *"links youth workers for encouragement, spiritual growth and sharing resources in order to expose every teenager to the gospel of Jesus Christ, establish them in a local church, and disciple them to help reach the world."*[105] Youth Specialties, located in El Cajon, California has been providing youth ministry resources and training since 1970. They now serve over 100,000 volunteer and career youth workers with materials, training, retreats, and the *Youthworker Journal*.[106]

There is much to learn about youth ministry from professionals in the hearing world. These youth ministry experts may not understand Deaf-World but those in Deaf ministry greatly benefit from the collective experience of these colleagues. Take every opportunity to learn, grow and share. Use general youth ministry resources and modify them to fit the needs of Deaf teenagers. Those of us involved in ministry with Deaf teenagers should not let anything prevent us from learning and improving. The more we know, the more we are able to adapt this general youth ministry information and resources to the Deaf culture, language and mind. This is much easier with the people who are part of the New Culture of Deafness as seen in this next generation. We must be diligent about seeking the best youth ministry resources possible. God will use the resources to bolster our knowledge and skills as we strive to reach Deaf teenagers with the gospel.

Personal Narrative ———————————————————— Chad Entinger

Nathaniel is one cool teenager! He is a bit tall and has brown, wavy hair. He dons cool glasses and has the confident walk of a leader. His clothing reflects the creativity of his generation of youth.

Nathaniel is Deaf. He was born Deaf. One of his trademark moves is to present hearing people he meets with a business card. On the business card reads, "I am Deaf." Nathaniel belongs to a unique cultural group of people known as "D"eaf people. He is not ashamed of being Deaf; he is proud.

Nathaniel is young. He feels and knows he is a part of the youth culture. Being involved in activities with other peers his age gives him a sense of belonging. He has participated in drama productions with other hearing teenagers. During the summer, Nathaniel energetically and enthusiastically participates in camps for youth. Nathaniel takes much joy in simply hanging out with his fellow peers.

Nathaniel travels extensively with his parents, who are missionaries. He is a respected part of his family, as his parents and siblings use sign language to communicate. Nathaniel, apparently, enjoys being a part of his family and participating in the activities they do together as a family.

Nathaniel is Deaf, young, and a vital part of his family.

Because Nathaniel is respected as a Deaf person, as a young person, and as a valuable member of his family, he has become a tremendous Christian leader who influences other Deaf Teenagers for Jesus.

We all are multi-cultural. Yet, we all serve the ONE God.

Discussion and Review

Vision IMPACT
Chapter 8—Ministry with Teenagers

Expressions

Who influenced you most in becoming a Christian? How did this occur and what role did this person or persons play in your life? Relational ministry means "earning the right" to share the most important message in the world. What does this mean to you? If you are familiar with the *Youth For Christ* or *Young Life* ministries, give a description of what you have seen or experienced.

Challenge

What are examples of activities that would be fun for most teenagers? Why is it important for Christian outreach to be fun? How is a Christian outreach different from a "Christian Deaf Club"? Why are the volunteer leaders so important to this ministry?

What happens if a teenager you are reaching out to doesn't accept Jesus as Lord and Savior? Do you continue the friendship? How?

Why is it important to have a diverse team of leaders?

Scripture

"We loved you so much that we were delighted to share with you not only the gospel of God but our lives as well, because you had become so dear to us." 1 Thessalonians 2:8

The First and Second Waves also maintained this characteristic of ministries based on love. What does it mean to "share with you…our lives as well" because of how much one is cherished? Why is it even more important in the Third Wave to develop a relational ministry outreach to Deaf teenagers?

Application

What are some of the elements of the First and Second Waves that still help meet the needs of today's Deaf teenagers? What negative traits of either era do we need to avoid in today's ministry? What do you see as the most important need of teenagers? How could you personally help?

Chapter 9—The DTQuest
Model

DTQuest brings together the best of youth and Deaf ministry to reach a new generation of Deaf and hard of hearing with the gospel of Jesus Christ.

Upon graduation from seminary, Kathy and I moved to Gainesville, Georgia where I had accepted a teaching position. We did not know anyone who lived in the area other than people we had met during the interview process. After visiting some churches, we attended the First Baptist Church and noticed they had a sign language interpreter. Kathy and I knew a few rudimentary signs. At the end of of the service, we went down front and met Charles and Janie Penland, a Deaf couple, who became our first and best friends in Gainesville. Charles grew up in Georgia and Janie in Tennessee. Both attended the residential schools for the Deaf. We spent hundreds of hours together as close friends. We met and spent time with many other Deaf friends. We were soaking up the Deaf-World and language of the Deaf. We were involved together in a church start and various ministry experiences. Charles and I took six Deaf teenage boys to a Young Life camp in the summer of 1991. Janie and I taught sign language classes together. I baptized their daughter, Lindsay. Their son, Chip, who is now the pastor of a Deaf church, grew up in front of our eyes. Our souls were woven together and they ushered us into Deaf-World. Sadly, Janie passed away suddenly and unexpectedly in 1993. This was such an incredible loss. We moved from Gainesville to Louisville, Kentucky in 1994, but the Penlands continue to be wonderful friends and an important part of our lives.

It is interesting to look back and see how God works. During my last year of seminary, I had a class called "Supervised Ministry Experience" where I was required to write six competency statements. On September 14, 1982, I wrote as one of my goals, "I will participate with a group of young people in developing a mission comitment to the deaf. The first part of the experience is to learn the basic skills of sign language together."[107] God knew we had a lot to learn and all the changes in Deaf-World that were to come. Eighteen years later, in the year 2000, in the fullness of time, Kathy and I incorporated DeafYouth Ministries for this purpose. This mission of DeafYouth Ministries is to reach Deaf and hard of hearing teenagers with the gospel of Jesus

Christ. DeafYouth Ministries/DTQuest is based on over two decades of youth and Deaf ministry experience[108].

—*Bob Ayres*

DeafYouth Ministries, was established in 2000 to *"bringing together the best of youth and Deaf ministry"* in reaching Deaf teenagers for Christ. The heart of the ministry is the local relational outreach called *DTQuest* (DeafTeen Quest). Everything we do is designed to involve Deaf teenagers in life-changing relationships with caring, Christian adults who help them understand the truth of Jesus Christ. In the *fullness of time* God called this ministry into existence to help craft a path for establishing *sustainable* Third Wave Deaf ministries.

DeafYouth Ministries/DTQuest works diligently to put these principles in action. We recognize the challenges of responding to the needs of this next generation. We make an effort to put forth the highest quality logos and materials that appeal to this generation of young people. The summer camps utilize lights, loud music, video, drama, and other high-energy events to communicate the relevance of the gospel. At the annual *Deaf Teen Ministry National Symposium*, we try to showcase the cutting-edge of technology, Deaf-Music, drama, and video so others will carry this value back into the local communities. But without question, it is the simplest piece of the puzzle that is the heart of the ministry; loving, prayerful, committed Christian adults willing to work as a team in developing authentic ministry relationships with Deaf teenagers through the local DTQuest affiliates.

There are three basic aspects of DeafYouth Ministries. Our first (and most important) goal is to set up local DTQuest ministries through like-minded evangelical ministries such as *Youth For Christ* and *Young Life*. The local DTQuest ministry is completely part of the mission of the sponsoring ministry; we are just a resource for helping them fulfill their mission to reach *every* teen with the gospel. Second, we provide training for DTQuest leaders through the annual national symposium and regional opportunities. The third part of the ministry is the summer camping and missions programs that are designed to strengthen the local ministry.

The common name DTQuest (Deaf Teen Quest) creates a national network that strengthens the ministry of the local outreach. The importance of using the same ministry name is in direct response to the Deaf Diaspora. This creates a "net" that gives Deaf teenagers a connection with other young Deaf Christians from across the country. Imagine the scenario at Gallaudet or the National Institute for the Deaf (NTID) where two Christian Deaf college students pass each other in the hall. One is wearing a Young Life shirt and the other a YFC logo on their ball cap. They may not even take notice of each other. But if they both have DTQuest logos (an organization established specifically for them and other Deaf teenagers), even though one is sponsored by Young Life and the other by Youth For Christ, their eyes widen as they meet. *"Wow! You involved DTQuest? Cool. Where?"* One is from Maryland and the other from Indiana, but the connection is made. Would they recognize the name Deaf Institute, Christ United Methodist or Sunset Presbyterian? No. But they would recognize DTQuest, which is sponsored in individual areas by each of these three ministries. As described in the first section of this book, Deaf teenagers are so scattered that no one denomination or even para-church organization can effectively reach them. By creating this network of like-minded ministries with a passion for the gospel and love for Deaf teenagers, we are able to reach the largest number of Deaf teenagers possible. Our slogan is, "Embracing God's vision for reaching Deaf teenagers."

Since there are multiple DTQuest affiliates with different sponsoring ministries, the area name is used when promoting the local ministry. For example, this first area was *DTQuest-Greater Louisville* not just *DTQuest*. This is important to use the area's name when promoting local activities. Teenagers or their families may become confused when they are connected with multiple areas. This is particularly important when a teenager attends the residential school for the Deaf but lives in a different part of the state.

The benefits of DTQuest affiliation
Support and Guidance Provided for the Area Coordinator

Sample Training Subjects
- The Fundraising Role of the Area Coordinator
- The Role of the Area Coordinator in Leadership Training
- The Basics of Taking Teens to Camps
- Taking Care of Yourself…emotionally, spiritually and intellectually.
- Understanding Denominational Differences
- Recruiting and Incorporating New Leaders
- Mentoring for the Area Coordinator
- Building a Strong Steering Committee

Training Opportunities for Staff and Volunteers
- Deaf Teen Ministry National Symposium (annually)
- Mid-year Regional Training

- Information about other training opportunities
- Training to address specific area needs as they arise

National Standards of Excellence

- National accountability and cooperation for consistent, effective relational ministry
- Avoid a sense of isolation and burn-out
- Helps local areas maintain a focus on the gospel of Jesus Christ, helping teens develop a love for Scripture as authority in one's life, and the establishment of opportunities for service and leadership.

National Recognition of Name and Ministry

- DTQuest was created specifically for Deaf and hard of hearing teenagers in the 21st Century.
- DTQuest is based on the best models of both Deaf and Youth ministry.
- There is an instant recognition of like-minded ministries from across the country because of the common name and logo.
- DeafYouth Ministries is constantly promoting DTQuest on a national level.

Fundraising Support

- Development of "Buy My Silence!" fundraiser for local areas
- DTConnect is a way to develop local support for fundraising/awareness events.
- DeafYouth Ministries is working on national grants that will provide local and national support.
- There is an open sharing of fundraising ideas among the affiliates

Training Materials

- The "Blue Book" for potential new leaders
- "Orientation for New Leaders"—four sessions
- "Leadership Training"—eight sessions
- *Deaf Diaspora: The Third Wave of Deaf Ministry*
- *Real-Life Wisdom: Stories for the Road* (general ministry help)

- Information about other training resources material and workshops
- Development of new ministry resources

Summer Camping Program

- DTQuest Camp—a basic introduction to Jesus Christ
- GROWcamp—helping teens deepen their faith
- Mission trips for Deaf teenagers
- Backpacking/Wilderness Trips
- Weekend retreats for discipleship

What Do We Ask of You?

- **Excellence** in all you do.
- **Compliance** with our standards of excellence and expectations for ongoing leadership training.
- **Commitment** to working in support of your sponsoring ministry. You are an important part of their outreach to reach *every* teenager.
- **Communication**—regular, honest communication with us about your needs, questions, concerns, and feedback.
- **Responsibility** for your role on the leadership team. The entire team is accountable for functioning as the Body of Christ and working together to reach teens for Christ.
- **Willingness** to adhere to the Christian principles and expected behavior for leaders. We expect you to be an active part of the local church.
- **Fiscal management**—honest, acceptable record-keeping supervised by a steering committee to make sure every penny in-and-out is accounted.
- **Faithfulness** to the gospel, to the mission, and to each other. Although working with Deaf teenagers is a lot of fun, it is serious business and very challenging. This ministry remains totally dependent on the Spirit of God for every task.

Responsibilities of the Area Coordinator

Each DTQuest area has an Area Coordinator who is the primary person responsible for the local ministry. She or he is responsible for making sure the local ministry follows the guidelines established by both DeafYouth Ministries and the sponsoring ministry. Basically, DeafYouth Ministries establishes rules and guidelines for the national ministry. The sponsoring local ministry agrees to, and enforces, these rules and guidelines (and may have some of their own). The Area Coordinator is responsible for making sure rules and guidelines are followed by volunteer leaders in the local ministry. The Area Coordinator has the most important role.

There are four primary responsibilities for the Area Coordinator: **leadership, management, events, and outreach.**[109] Each area is unique so the demands of the position will vary. These responsibilities will be described in terms of percentages. Some affiliates (and times of the year) will require a shift in these percentages. This is only a guide for your benefit.

The following principles are important to apply for this ministry to be sustainable. The first is to develop a *team* of leaders for ministry. This is where the majority of the Area Coordinator's time is spent. The second is to think in terms of a large geographic area. Deaf teenagers are scattered geographically. The third is to understand the secular nature of the average Deaf teen. This is not a "Club for Christians." It is a Christian outreach to all Deaf and hard of hearing teens.

Leadership—50%
Recruiting, Training, and Supervising Leaders
The basic components of leadership are recruiting, training, and supervising volunteer leaders. You are the facilitator of the team. We follow the model described in the Romans 12 regarding the body of Christ. Jesus is the Head and we each serve in accordance with our gifts. We need great diversity and greater unity as we become a team. Applying these truths involves the majority of your time. The first duty of the Area Coordinator is to make sure no one is working with teenagers who might be a danger to them. This is why all leaders are screened and all must attend regular training and meetings. At least half of your time is spent on leadership related issues.

Events—20%
Planning Outreach and Discipleship Events

The core of DTQuest is the monthly outreach events. This involves activities such as rock-climbing, bowling, swimming, skiing, hiking, etc. The goal is to provide good, healthy fun, create opportunities for positive interactions, and build a sense of community. Sometime during each event is the *Gathering*. The format is about 45—60 minutes and may include team-building games, announcements, music, video, skits, dramatization of a Scripture story, as well as a presentation of some aspect of Jesus' life and application to their daily lives. The other events that involve an Area Coordinator's time are weekend or summer camps, GROWgroups and mission trips. This is why building a team is so vital. One person cannot do it all.

Management—10%
Administrative Responsibilities and Networking

The Area Coordinator is the main liaison with the sponsoring ministry. You will need to communicate regularly with this ministry and seek support and advice. DeafYouth Ministries serves as a support for you. Our only authority is to monitor compliance with our affiliation agreement made with the sponsoring ministry. Communication is vital. Another important aspect of this part of the job is maintaining a positive relationship with the schools, local churches and deaf ministries, and other outreach ministries. Record keeping is not a particularly fun part of any ministry but it is important to maintain a good database and follow standard accounting procedures. It is also important to spend time in ongoing training and development of new skills.

Outreach—20%
Personal Ministry with Deaf Teenagers and their Families

The Area Coordinator models effective relational ministry for the team. An individual leader can only maintain significant influence in the lives of a few teenagers. One key to sustainable ministry is the importance of each team member doing his or her part. The relationship with a teenager includes their family. This means spending time with teens as a group and individually. Leaders attend events and ceremonies that are important to the teens. Find a common interest with the teenagers and spend time together. This is the core of effective relational ministry. You are part of a team of leaders who each have significant ministry relationships with Deaf and hard of hearing teenagers.

The Area Coordinator…

1) works under the supervision of the sponsoring ministry.
2) works in cooperation with the standards established by DeafYouth Ministries.
3) provides leadership, training and accountability for all volunteers.
4) reaches out to all Deaf teenagers regardless of their style of communication.
5) works cooperatively with other mainstream denominations and non-denominational groups for the stated goals of this agreement.
6) builds a team of Deaf, hard of hearing, and hearing adults who are morally sound and work together as the body of Christ.
7) is supportive of the family of Deaf teenagers and their denominations, even if they do not personally agree with the choices of the family.

DTQuest Leadership

DTQuest leaders are Christian adults who are trained and supervised by the Area Coordinator with support from the sponsoring ministry. Many of the training resources are provided by DeafYouth Ministries. The sponsoring ministry agrees to provide background checks, interviews and references to ensure the highest quality of leadership. Leaders must agree to our statement of faith and personal behavior standards, and be involved in regular leadership training and supervision.

> *"For by the grace given me I say to every one of you: Do not think of yourself more highly than you ought, but rather think of yourself with sober judgment, in accordance with the measure of faith God has given you. Just as each of us has one body with many members, and these members do not all have the same function, so in Christ we who are many form one body, and each member belongs to all the others."* Romans 12:3-5, NIV

Probably the most challenging part of DTQuest is building a team that is diverse and united. It is critical that we understand the importance of having Deaf, hard of hearing, and hearing, as well as young, middle and older people of various ethnic groups working together for the glory of Jesus Christ! It also has practical benefits for reaching the diverse population of Deaf teenagers. One type of person is not more important than another although each has different gifts and connections. An important part of being a DTQuest leader is a humble spirit and willingness to become part of this united team of leaders.

DTQuest leaders must be people who…

- have a personal relationship with Jesus Christ as Savior and Lord.

- maintain appropriate and respectful interactions at all times.

- live Biblical lifestyles that do not include homosexual, extra-marital, or pre-marital sexual relations.

- do not have a substance abuse or alcohol addiction unless this individual is in recovery and under supervision.

- have not been involved in any type of criminal activity that involved violence, drugs, or any type of sexual misconduct.

- have not have been the subjects of any disciplinary action, in any setting, that involved mistreatment of children.

- do not view pornography and are not involved in any pornographic or illicit activity.

- do not have a criminal background; the sponsoring ministry shall perform an appropriate criminal background check and interview of their leaders.

- will respond to any reports by a teen regarding harming him/herself or others, committing a crime, or is being abused.

- report to the sponsoring ministry any suspected or observed misconduct by other volunteer leaders.

DeafYouth Ministries makes no apology for following the Scriptures with regards to personal behavior for leaders. We expect leaders to be positive role models in the lives of young people. If a leader has been involved with personal immoral behavior in the past but has now repented and strives to live a moral life, then adequate time, counseling and appropriate supervision of the adult should be given before allowing him or her to be considered for a volunteer leadership position.

DTQuest creates a positive environment for Deaf teenagers, but is also designed to provide an opportunity to mature in faith. Everything is designed to create situations where you as a leader are able to have deeper discussions with teenagers about spiritual issues. This is where sign language skills and sensitivity to Deaf culture are critical. Deaf teenagers need to be able to explore in-depth spiritual discussions with minimal or no barriers. The outreach events include a serious and sequential presentation of the gospel. Leaders must always be tuned in to teenagers. The most important part of the ministry is one-on-one time with Deaf teenagers (of the same gender) to develop quality ministry relationships. Be sensitive to the importance of confidentiality and privacy in these interactions but remember you are part of a team and there are times and situations for sharing about these conversations with the other members of the ministry team. Discussions within the team must remain confidential as well, unless there is a compelling reason for seeking outside professional help.

Relational ministry involves spending time with teenagers in their world. Show personal interest in them. Attend their sporting events. Show up at their practices. Get together for fun times. Send them a congratulatory note or card when appropriate. This is referred to in many circles as *Contact Time*. It means investing your time in the things that teenagers themselves care about. Use these experiences to build stronger relationships with two to three teens. Teens need to know that leaders like them and enjoy their friendship. A DTQuest leader is not *just* a friend; she or he is responsible to behave as a positive Christian adult influence. Have fun. Be wild and crazy at times but always remember your influence in the lives of Deaf teenagers. Your behavior should always point them towards Christ. The Area Coordinator will guide the ministry team in building these ministry relationships. Working as part of a team of leaders is a vital aspect of effective outreach ministry.

Evangelical Perspective—DTQuest directs young people to a Biblical understanding of the person of Jesus Christ as found in the four gospels. The teachings of local affiliates of DTQuest must be in line with the teachings of the Old and New Testaments and leaders must be comfortable with an "uncluttered" evangelical faith based in Scripture. We believe that salvation is a gift of grace given by God to a repentant heart. One does not earn salvation. *"So, you will be saved, if you honestly say, 'Jesus is Lord,' and if you believe with all your heart that God raised him from death. God will accept you and save you, if you truly believe this and tell it to others."* (Romans 10:9-10, CEV). We recognize the differences in various churches and discourage any focus on those things that divide us along denominational or doctrinal lines. DTQuest is focused on teens developing a personal relationship with God through Jesus Christ, and maturing in their faith. We believe the simple profession of faith given by Apostle Peter in Matthew 16:16 is the foundation upon which the Church is built, *"You are the Christ, the son of the Living God."* We each have different perspectives about the fundamental elements of salvation but the basic faith is about the redemption of our lives through the goodness of God. As young people mature, the goal is for them to connect with local churches to deepen their theological study and understanding.

Supporting Family—There are so many assaults on the family in today's society and it is a high priority of DeafYouth Ministries/DTQuest to support the family of Deaf teenagers. This is a vital part of our identity. Everything we do should be geared towards building and strengthening a teenager's relationship within their family unit. Even if a teenager has parents who are not Christians, it is still important to respect the vital role of parents in a young person's life. Our agenda is not to promote one particular communication style, denomination, or to try and "fix" the family. It is certainly never an effort to replace the primary role of the family. DTQuest is specifically an outreach to Deaf and hard of hearing teenagers and should not lose focus on this population group. Parents are always welcomed to any event as observers, and various events are designed to include the family. DTQuest itself is not for all ages and not for hearing teens. Hearing teenagers (including CODAs) have many options and Deaf teens have very few. A Deaf teen may invite a hearing teen friend to visit but DTQuest should always remain a Deaf experience. The events are geared towards teenagers and designed to minister specifically to Deaf teenagers.

Interaction with schools—Because of the nature of outreach to Deaf teenagers, it is important to maintain a respectful and positive relationship with educators and the school system. Many of the DTQuest leaders will also be in roles as interpreters and teachers with the Deaf. DTQuest volunteers and staff should maintain the highest level of integrity. Effective lifestyle evangelism in academic settings is always sensitive to ethical codes of conduct. Outside of the public school setting, one can more openly share personal faith but this may not be appropriate within the school. Through the quality of relationships, people will be attracted to the activities of DTQuest.

The schools can be of help in sharing information about DTQuest activities to students although they cannot legally share mailing lists or other personal information about students to outside groups. You must earn their trust and maintain their confidence by being trustworthy. Schools have an obligation to make Deaf youth and their families aware of any opportunities for positive social and personal interaction including those of a religious nature. By law, they are not supposed to exclude religious information from distribution. DTQuest is one such opportunity and should be included along with other social and educational activities.

The DTQuest activities should generally meet in places other than school, depending on the setting and culture of the school. Please be sensitive to the pressures that public school administrators work under regarding this issue. Build quality relationships with the administration and teachers so they will speak positively about you to others. Promote the idea that DTQuest is a place where Deaf teenagers can find a positive peer group and interact with postive adult role models. DTQuest is one of the community supports in the life of the teenager.

Other Interested Adults—One of the challenges of this ministry is addressing the needs of young adults. Although DTQuest is specifically focused on teenagers, we recognize the wisdom in addressing the needs of Deaf young adults, without losing focus on our primary mission. This is a vital source of potential leaders. To avoid problems, young adults need proper training, discipleship and time before becoming DTQuest leaders and developing ministerial relationships with teens. Parents are always welcomed to visit at DTQuest. Other adults (including Steering Committee members) should *not* just show up at DTQuest events or Contact Time without direct permission of the Area Coordinator. Our first commitment is to ensure the safety of the teenagers. It is difficult for a teenager to determine who is *safe* and who is not; their assumption is that any adult with the DTQuest ministry is a person to be trusted. We have no control over further contact that these adults have with Deaf teens following the DTQuest event and so it is wise to use great caution. Some areas will send out an annual letter to the Deaf teenagers and their parents to identify exactly who the approved DTQuest leaders are for the coming school year. This is a particularly good idea if there is a past DTQuest leader, whom you have concerns about, who may continue to pretend he or she is associated with your local ministry.

Local Churches and Ministries—The overriding goal of this ministry is to partner with God in reaching Deaf teenagers and help disciple them to become mature believers. The foundation for Christian maturity is an understanding and respect for the authority of Scripture. GROWgroup is for deeper spiritual discussions in a small group setting; it is a Bible study that is applicable to the practical challenges facing teenagers. GROWgroup leaders are part of the regular leadership and involved with the overall ministry. GROWgroup should never be taught from a denominational perspective, although leaders may share personal beliefs. It is a place to learn how to grow in faith, assume roles of service and leadership and share faith with others. It should also encourage these teens to become more active in their churches and denominations.

One of the difficulties in being an interdenominational, non-sectarian ministry is the proper interaction with local churches. There is a great diversity of churches even within the same denomination. There are some denominations and religious groups that fundamentally do not agree with the mainstream Christian faith. There are cults and cult-like groups that are even dangerous. There are rigid, legalistic churches that may agree with the mainstream Christian faith theologically but are oppressive beyond reason. There are some religious groups that are clearly not Christian. There are churches with some unusual beliefs but are solid on the basic Christian faith. There are churches and individuals who will want to use DTQuest as an effort to *harvest* new members, therefore ignoring our commitment to support the family. This is unacceptable. In many instances, it is a subjective decision whether to involve a particular church or individual in DTQuest. The local DTQuest ministry will follow the policies of the sponsoring ministry regarding interactions with local churches and ministries.

Two ministries have emerged out of DTQuest but have different missions: Deaf Teen Connect (DTConnect) and Deaf Café. DTConnect is an informal network of Deaf ministries established to help local churches with Deaf ministry. These groups support the DTQuest concept but prefer to maintain a separate, denominationally-based ministry in cooperation with others. DTConnect will likely become part of the National Network of Youth Ministries. Deaf Café is an outreach ministry to young adults. Deaf Café originated out of DTQuest because of the concern for the absence of ministry for those who have graduated from high school and the application of DTQuest principles in reaching this young adult population.[110]

It is vital that the programming of Deaf Café maintain a clear separation from DTQuest students at least until these students graduate from high school, regardless of the age of the student. I am a strong supporter of Deaf Café and one of the conceptual architects of the program but it is an outreach to non-Christian young and middle-aged adults. Mixing non-Christian adults (including some with addiction and emotional problems) with high school students is a formula for disaster. This same policy should be considered with other Deaf ministries that bring together adults and teens. Traditionally, mixing together Deaf adults and young people was common because of the assumed positive influence on the children and youth. This assumption cannot be made anymore and Deaf ministries need to exercise extreme caution when planning intergenerational activities.

Frequently Asked Questions by Parents

Who sponsors DTQuest in my area?

Each area has a different sponsoring ministry but all agree to follow the same basic format and philosophy established by DeafYouth Ministries.

My child has a cochlear implant. Can she be involved with DTQuest?

Absolutely! We love Deaf and hard of hearing teens. The type of assistive technology used by the teen for hearing is the perogative of the family. This is not a concern for us.

My child doesn't sign well or not at all. Will this be a problem?

Any Deaf or hard of hearing teen is welcomed regardless of their signing skills. Our leaders sign a variety of styles and we try to be sensitive to each person's preference.

Is this one denomination's outreach?

No. Our leaders are from a variety of denominations. We first encourage the teens to get involved with your family's church and denomination. If you are interested, we can inform you about Deaf activities and churches in the area.

What if our family is not Christian?

All Deaf teens are welcomed! We believe it is important for teens to learn about God's love and the person of Jesus Christ. We never pressure teens about God in any way.

Can I come with my child to events?

Sure! Parents are always welcomed! Think of it like a Deaf youth group; activities are designed to appeal to Deaf teenagers, so it may be a little "wild and crazy," but come on!

I'm a parent of a Deaf teen. Can I volunteer to be a DTQuest leader?

Absolutely, as long as you are in agreement with the other requirements of leadership. Talk to the Area Coordinator. Parents are an important part of the ministry team.

Frequently Asked Questions by Volunteer Leaders

What is Relational Ministry?

Christian adult leaders develop ministry relationships with teenagers to help them grow spiritually, emotionally, and socially.

What is an "outreach" ministry?

The monthly DTQuest outreach events are designed for leaders to bring teenagers who are not yet involved in church or Bible study. It is a time to focus on the teens and build relationships with them. Leaders should be working like a team to make sure every teen in attendance gets individual attention.

How do I develop relationships with teenagers?

DTQuest is a program; relationships occur one-to-one. DTQuest leaders should make it a priority to attend activities of the teens they know and also meet new teens. You become a positive influence in their lives. Ask questions about spiritual things, when appropriate. Involve Christian teenagers in regular Bible studies such as the GROWgroup.

Is the Internet a good place to meet teenagers?

Absolutely not! The Internet is a good place to communicate information. We all know the dangers of adults in contact with children and adolescents on the Internet. It also makes these teenagers more vulnerable to other adults with bad intentions if they develop a habit of meeting people on-line.

Should I recruit teenagers and families to MY church?

No. Our first effort is to connect teens with their family's church, if they belong to one. If they have no previous connection, our next step is to help them consider churches within their own denomination unless the family expresses a clear interest in other options.

What if they are still looking for a church?

Let them know about other options, including your church. We want them and their families to connect with local churches but not any one particular church or denomination.

Why is it important to have a diverse leadership team?

God is reaching out to Deaf teens through DTQuest by bringing people together from various backgrounds. Each leader has different gifts and will connect with different teens. This enables the ministry to reach out to more teens with various interests and personalities.

What about my personal life?

When you become a DTQuest leader, you become a minister of the gospel and are called to a higher standard of living. This means others will look at your life more closely. Be aware of your behavior, especially in front of young Christians and non-Christians, who may be easily confused.

Can I bring other adults to the outreach activities?

No. A teen does not recognize the difference between an approved DTQuest leader and any other adult who attends. The Area Coordinator may decide to invite someone to visit such as a local Deaf minister who is known and trusted.

As a DTQuest leader, can I bring my children to DTQuest events?

No. There may be occasional exceptions but the focus of the events is on the teenagers and you want to have as few distractions as possible.

Can leaders spend time with students of the opposite sex?

This is strongly discouraged. Feelings and emotions can confuse and complicate relationships. We also want to protect you from accusations of immoral behavior. Avoid being in any compromising situation. Discuss any concerns with the Area Coordinator.

What is the dating policy for DTQuest leaders?

Healthy boundaries are crucial. DTQuest leaders may never date students. Dating confuses the feelings of the teenager and creates awkward and compromising relationships. A DTQuest leader may date another leader but needs to use good judgment in the relationship so as not to negatively impact the DTQuest ministry or leadership.

Can "hearing" friends or family of the teens attend the DTQuest events?

Yes, but only as a support the Deaf teen in his or her friendships and by invitation of the teen. DTQuest is always a "Deaf" event and should never lose this focus.

Can I just lead a GROWgroup Bible study but not participate in outreach events?

No. GROWgroup leaders are regular leaders and expected to participate in outreach opportunities. This includes attendance at any leadership meetings.

How long does it take to become a DTQuest leader?

Every leader should go through orientation before any contact with teens. A student who has graduated from high school must spend at least one year away from DTQuest activities for middle and high school students before beginning leadership. During this year, they should continue to grow in their faith through church involvement and study.

Establishing a DTQuest Affiliate

You may be thinking, *"Where do I start? Which ministry would make the best sponsor of DTQuest?"* If you already know a potential sponsoring ministry that meets the criteria given by DeafYouth Ministries, provide them with a copy of this book, *Deaf Diaspora: The Third Wave of Deaf Ministry.* Make sure they understand the responsibilities for sponsoring this ministry. It is a community-wide outreach and will require involvement by para-church organizations and churches of various denominations. The question for sponsorship of DTQuest is the willingness to cooperate with others from different perspectives to reach unchurched and non-Christian Deaf youth. Generally, the easiest fit for sponsorship of DTQuest is *Young Life* or *Youth For Christ.*

If you are an individual interested in starting an affiliation, first meet with others in your area who are already involved with Deaf ministry. Also, meet with area ministries like *Youth For Christ, Young Life, Fellowship of Christian Athletes, Campus Crusade for Christ,* and *Navigators.* Find out if there are others in your area who share a similar sense of calling or already offer an outreach to Deaf teenagers. Talk with your church about their interest and willingness to help fund a basic budget for this relational outreach.

Ask yourself these questions...Is there a spirit of cooperation or competition in our community? Would this be a duplication of another like-minded ministry in the area? Is there one particular organization that seems most appropriate for sponsorship or should it be a consortium of ministries who sign the affiliation agreement? Will such an effort truly benefit the effectiveness of the local ministries? Then, get in touch with DeafYouth Ministries. We will help connect you with others in your area with a common interest. We can then put together a plan for starting the ministry in your local area.

Starting a New Area

Step 1	Pray without ceasing and follow God's leading.
Step 2	Learn about the resources in your area and nationally.
Step 3	Think in the long term; create sustainable ministry.
Step 4	Always keep your "radar" up for potential new leaders.
Step 5	Meet with potential leaders to share your vision and learn theirs.
Step 6	Cooperate with existing Deaf ministries, even if they are not involved.
Step 7	Make friends with the school personnel; help them see the social and educational benefits of DTQuest.
Step 8	Take Deaf teens with you to visit existing DTQuest ministries.
Step 9	Decide on your approach; GROWgroup first or Outreach first?
Step 10	Go for it! Provide a quality product and trust God for the results.

Accountability—It is required that each DTQuest program have a local sponsoring ministry and Area Coordinator. This provides accountability, liability coverage, and a formal relationship for fulfilling the requirements of the contract. If an affiliate strays from the stated values and principles of DeafYouth Ministries, this allows us to help address the problem. If the issue is not resolvable, our only direct power is the ability to void the contract and prevent usage of the program names by this organization (such as DTQuest and GROWgroup). We have no direct authority over the local affiliates other than determining the requirements for being an affiliate. This protects all the affiliates who use the common program names from poor decisions made by any one affiliate. Ultimately, it provides a better quality program for Deaf teenagers and their families.

Fiscal Responsibilities—Fiscal concerns of an affiliation are the responsibility of the sponsoring ministry. All standard and acceptable accounting regulations apply. DeafYouth Ministries is not responsible for any errors or omissions in fiscal management by an affiliate. DeafYouth Ministries may request financial reports from affiliates. Proper management of donated funds is expected by any sponsoring ministry. This is another important reason for having a responsible sponsoring ministry. Local management is the responsibility of the sponsoring ministry.

There must be someone who is specifically responsible for the programs. This person is the Area Coordinator and is accountable to the sponsoring ministry and agreements made with DeafYouth Ministries. We may provide training opportunities, resources, information, events, etc. but the day-to-day management of the affiliate is the responsibility of the sponsoring ministry. We have the right to ask for program reports but do not provide direct supervision to paid or unpaid staff, or volunteers.

Fund Raising—The local area is responsible for raising its own funds. These funds are managed through the sponsoring ministry. Types of fund raising activities should be described and included in the program and financial reports to DeafYouth Ministries. All fund raising will be in compliance with local, State and Federal laws. It is assumed that local areas will choose fund raising ideas that are morally and ethically acceptable. Occasionally, someone will come up with an idea that seems reasonable but has serious flaws. When in doubt, please contact DeafYouth Ministries for consultation and feedback. Part of our ministry is to help affiliates avoid common pitfalls of nonprofit management and to provide assistance.

Reporting—Consistent reports to DeafYouth Ministries about the activities in local areas allow us to be supportive and provide effective feedback regarding our affiliation agreement. Regular reporting provides consistent contact with affiliates. It provides necessary information for designing camps, new programs, training, promotional and fund raising ideas. The role of DeafYouth Ministries is to help affiliates avoid common problems, find resources, and build sustainable ministry with Deaf teens. DeafYouth Ministries does not have direct control over local areas other than to require compliance to our agreement. **DeafYouth Ministries owns the DTQuest name and has the right to withdraw permission**

from using it from an area that is not in compliance with our agreement. Our goal is to protect the integrity of the common name and mission. Our prayer is to serve as a catalyst for effective and sustainable ministry to Deaf and hard of hearing teenagers.

Financial support of DeafYouth Ministries—We ask each area to help support DeafYouth Ministries by assisting us in acquiring funding from the annual mission budget of local churches. We do not charge an affiliation fee. This helps us provide support and training for local affiliates and help expand the ministry. This is our effort to build a sustainable ministry that has a lasting impact on the future of ministry with the Deaf community. It is very difficult to find funding for Deaf ministry. Many churches assume that Deaf people are attending church *somewhere* so they assume the responsibility lies elsewhere. These churches need to be educated on the importance of supporting Deaf ministry as a mission. Support of Deaf ministry should not be motivated by a church's desire to recruit new members but must come from a heart for missions. There is a basic budget for stability that we ask local areas to develop as they become an affiliate. Adequate funding has historically been one of the reasons it has been so difficult to establish sustainable Deaf ministries.

Learn more about DeafYouth Ministries/DTQuest on the web at www.dtquest.org

Discussion and Review

Vision IMPACT
Chapter 9—The DTQuest Model

Expressions

Think back on your teenage years. What are some of the most significant decisions you made during those times? Do you know anyone who had a difficult childhood but became a strong Christian leader during the teenage years? Why do you think those years are so important?

Challenge

Have you been to a DTQuest or similar outreach event? What are the aspects of the ministry designed specifically for them as *teenagers*? What is designed specifically for the *Deaf-Mind* of the teenager?

How do you see DTQuest reflect the priorities of the Third Wave?

DTQuest uses a common name to create national name recognition. The primary reason for use of a common name is to help Deaf teens stay connected with likeminded ministries if they move to new areas. Why might this be especially important in today's mobile society?

Scripture

"For God so loved the world that he gave his only Son, so that everyone who believes in him will not perish but have eternal life. God did not send his Son into the world to condemn it, but to save it. John 3:16-17

"Christ is the visible image of the invisible God. He existed before God made anything at all and is supreme over all creation." Colossians 1:15

Why is it especially important for Third Wave ministries to be focused primarily on Jesus?

Application

What are the advantages and disadvantages of affiliating with DeafYouth Ministries and establishing a local DTQuest?

Chapter 10—Conclusion

Do you not know? Have you not heard?
The Everlasting God, the LORD, the Creator of the ends of the earth
Does not become weary or tired. His understanding is inscrutable.
He gives strength to the weary, and to him who lacks might He increases power.
Though youths grow weary and tired, and vigorous young men stumble badly,
Yet those who wait for the LORD Will gain new strength;
They will mount up with wings like eagles,
They will run and not get tired,
They will walk and not become weary.
Isaiah 40:28-31

The Third Wave…The New Culture of Deafness…Relational Ministry…The Three Cultures of Deaf Teenagers…The Deaf Alarm…Deaf Diaspora…these are many new concepts but the same gospel of Jesus Christ.

At some point, there will be an end to the Third Wave and it will be judged in part by its response to the changes that have occurred during the latter part of the 20th Century but also by the values of creativity, flexibility, sustainability, and adaptability established for future eras. The Third Wave will be the foundation for our Deaf children to reach the world for Christ. We must always encourage them to reach for new heights and be sensitive to the leading of the Holy Spirit. Change will continue, but truth is eternal. Never ignore one for the other. Push the edge of excellence to continue to improve. As others have said, *the best youth ministry has yet to be done.* We can always improve and God deserves our best. Never be satisfied with *"good enough."* Pray, prepare and perform even greater things for the glory of our Lord, Jesus Christ.

A Fictional DTQuest Leader's Meeting

In Chapter Four, seven fictional Deaf teenagers who represent the New Culture of Deafness were described to you. There is Aleah, Bryan, Christina, Deon, Erica, Federico, and Gracie who represent a wide-range of backgrounds, ethnicities, educational settings, and diversity. It may help to refer back to the end of Chapter 4 to refresh your memory. Let me introduce you to their DTQuest leaders.

Harold Latino male; 28 years old; recent graduate of Southern Baptist seminary; grew up Deaf/Oral but learned to sign ASL as a young adult; Area Coordinator

Izzy African-American male; 35 years old; strong ASL skills and only attended residential schools; African Methodist Episcopal (AME).

June Korean-American female; 22 years old; grew up with manually-signed English but has developed limited ASL skills; Catholic.

Karen white female; 45 years old; parent of a Deaf teenager and has strong youth ministry background and decent signing; Lutheran.

Leonard white male; 30 years old; excellent ASL skills through interpreter training program; attends Vineyard church.

Mary white female; 26 years old; ministry student; Deaf education background with excellent signing skills; Assembly of God.

The regular DTQuest leader's meeting is on Friday nights in the home of Karen. It begins with a covered dish meal (although usually KFC chicken and potato chips are on the menu) at 6:30 p.m. Some arrive early and others eat elsewhere but by 7:15 p.m. all have gathered in the living room. These are all fictional characters and none is based solely on any one person. Any direct similarity is solely coincidental and unintended. These are representative characters. Everything in the dialogue is signed although it is written in English. Occasionally, glossing is used in this dialogue; glossing means using English words to describe ASL communication.

Harold Okay, we need to start. We have a lot to do and discuss. Mary, would you open our time with prayer?

Mary Sure. Let's pray. God, wow, thanks so much for our coming together tonight...We love you...We really want to serve you and want Deaf teens know you. Help us honor you...help us enjoy and learn much...help us become one, unified, in Jesus. Amen.

All Amen.

Harold Thanks. Tonight, we need to spend some time planning next week's outreach at the Waterfront Park but I wanted first to learn together from the Bible and discuss about recruiting teens for camp. We really need to encourage teens to be involved in fund raising to help pay for camp and divide up who to contact and so forth...but we can discuss this later. First, Leonard, you have been teaching us about

Jesus' miracles and some of the history of Jesus' time. Why don't you go ahead with the teaching...

Leonard Sure. Fine. Scripture from Mark 6:30-44. Story about Jesus taking fish and bread and feeding 5,000 people. We'll use some CBS (Chronological Bible Storying) and drama but first want to watch video. This is from Deaf Missions, called "Life of Christ" signed by Belinda McCleese. Wow. She is awesome, her communication skills are incredible.

(After watching the 3 minute video through twice, Leonard involves the team in acting out the miracle. Then, he passes out a handout that describes the setting of the miracle and descriptions of the various people involved. They conclude with discussing how God uses our willingness to be faithful to feed Deaf teenagers spiritual food. The group closes with prayer.)

One of the most common mistakes made by ministry teams is to neglect their own spiritual growth as a team. The best way to maintain loving relationships with each other is to make it a priority to learn together. There should always be a Bible study incorporated into the meeting but this can also include training on relational ministry skills, Biblical or denominational history, camp counselor training, a book study, or any numbers of other subjects that help the team grow spiritually and as a unit. The leadership meeting is not intended to become a substitution for involvement in a local church. Leadership meetings are a time of inspiration, unity, and personal growth. Prayer is obviously a critical part of the meeting and will be commented on following the next section of this fictional leader's meeting.

Leadership meeting is a time for growing and recognizing that DTQuest leaders are not going to agree on every theological point. There are certainly some items that are "non-negotiable" but for the most part, we know that each member of the team comes from a different background and may attend churches in different denominations (such as this team does). The meeting is not the place to argue theological differences but it is a place to share insights and perspectives that may likely be diverse. Individual concerns should be resolved more privately with the awareness (and possible involvement) of the Area Coordinator. Stay focused on the basic Truth of Jesus Christ as found in the four gospels.

Let's continue with the meeting...

Leonard Next week, we'll begin with 3-Story Evangelism training. Mary and June went to training with Youth For Christ. It is an awesome way for teaching young people and leaders how to share their faith as they build relationships with others.

June   Yeah! I learned a ton! Mary and I will lead this over the next month or so of leadership. I think you'll all really enjoy it. It's very cool.

Harold   Great! Let's chat some now about camp. Karen, you've had some conversations with Aleah's and Gracie's parents?

Karen   Yeah, Gracie is good to go but Aleah's mom is still uncertain about the basketball camp schedule. Oh! I made a break-through with Federico's parents. I ran into them at a soccer game recently and had a great conversation. I think they were mostly concerned about Federico feeling uncomfortable because he doesn't really sign. I told them that we love Deaf teens and respect the family's communication preferences. I felt like we connected. Of course, Erica's fine and Deon's going.

Izzy   Who are we missing?

Mary   Let's see, Bryan, Christina...oh, I heard about two more Deaf brothers that just moved to the Southside.

Izzy   Really? Mainstreamed or residential?

Mary   I think they moved here from Maryland in the heart of Deaf-World. One of the members of the Deaf church told me about them.

Izzy   I live out that way and I can contact them. Let me see if I can find a connection. When I was at Gallaudet, I volunteered at MSSD and also some at MSD. I may recognize them.

June   Cool. Oh, there is an open-captioned movie at the theatre on Friday. Maybe we could meet some more teens there. Also, this Saturday is Deaf Social night at the food court of the Mall. Harold and I are going.

Karen   Someone needs to reach out to Bryan. I can't really do it since I'm an old hearing woman *(everyone chuckles)* but maybe Izzy, you could take Bryan with you to meet the new boys and spend some time with him. Even if Bryan doesn't come to GROWgroup, we need to keep spending time with him in his environment.

Harold   Right! Exactly right. Building a relationship with him outside of DTQuest will...hopefully...make him more interested in coming with you to an event. Regardless, if he never comes to DTQuest, you can still strengthen that relationship.

June   Yeah! You listen to his story and share your story and God's story with him. We are called to minister in Jesus' name and Jesus met people on their own turf. We need to do the same.

Izzy   I want to get with him for a Coke or maybe shoot some hoops with him. I don't know what's up with him but I think his family may be going through some tough times financially. I can hang around and chat with his mom when I get with him.

Mary   I think he is just hanging around the house this summer. Let's really work on getting him to camp. And I'm supposed to hang out with Christina next Wednesday. She is going to a birthday party at her cousin's house and invited me to go. I know enough Spanish to communicate basic information with her parents.

(The group continues to discuss camp details and fund raising to help teens afford camp. June suggested they take a moment to pray for the teens before going on and the group gratefully takes a moment to pray for each teen by name.)

Ministry with Deaf teenagers is quite difficult for a number of reasons and requires a more intentional approach than other youth ministries. This team of leaders works together as the Body of Christ, recognizing that communication within a ministry team is vital. Caution must always be exercised regarding confidentiality. We are crossing so many cultures to reach these teenagers with the gospel; there must be wise interactions with the family unit that involve multiple team members. People who serve in dual roles as sign language interpreters and are also on the ministry team must be *very* careful about divulging confidential information. Draw a sharp and clean line between your role as an interpreter and your role as a minister. Those who are not in this dual role can exercise more freedom in sharing observations and related information. However, it is still critical that ALL information shared stays within the ministry team and does not enter into the information highway.

There is a philosophy in youth ministry that states we should never start programming until our leaders know a large number of teenagers on a first-name basis. In Deaf-World, this number may be a low as ten Deaf teenagers. The point is that relational ministry must be completely about relationships. A lousy program with excellent relationships is much better than an excellent program with lousy relationships. Of course, excellence in both the program and relationships is the goal. If you already have a number of one-on-one relationships with Deaf teenagers, then your program will be successful. These relationships only occur if the team is working together, in support of the family, and to the glory of God.

The meeting continues…

Harold Anything else on camp? Okay, let's chat some about this month's DTQuest outreach. This will be a great opportunity to invite the new boys we heard about and also keep connecting with new teens. Last month, we had three new teens visit. That was very cool. We've got to keep going out where they are and getting to know them in their worlds. They are scattered all over.

Izzy Yeah, I'm giving the message this month on "Christian's LOVE"…last month was "Jesus CONNECTS"…and I am using the Scripture from Mark the Tenth chapter where James and John want to have a special place in the kingdom of God and Jesus says, "You must serve others."

Mary Oh! I know a game that will fit that well. It involves carrying people across an imaginary line. I can tie that together with serving others.

Karen This is paintball, right? Will we have a room at the place?

June Oh yeah, and we need to make sure everyone under eighteen has a parent permission form signed.

Harold We have a room to meet; I checked with the owner and they are also giving us a discount on drinks. I also sent out permission forms with the flyer. We did this last year and the teens loved it. I think Deon's father may even come with us. He loves paintball. I don't think Deon's parents are Christians. This will be great for him to hear the message as well.

Leonard Yeah, I don't mind voicing for him in the back of the room. I don't have any responsibility this month.

Karen Okay, transportation should be fine. I'll take my van.

June That holds five teens and two leaders and then I can take a couple of teens in my car. I've been wanting to spend some time with Erica *(Karen's daughter)*, so maybe she can ride with me.

Izzy Okay, so we have the game, the message…are we going to do any music?

Mary I don't mind leading that "Need You"[111] song we learned at summer camp. The teens loved it. Actually, Aleah and Christina were signing it the other day at GROWgroup. I can get them to lead it. We can do it without the rhythm track. It's not a big deal.

Izzy Cool. I can tie that back into the Scripture about how our need for God helps us be more forgiving of others who are also struggling.

Harold Well, it's getting late and we want to get to Aleah's softball game. It worked out this week because she has a late game. We'll see everyone on Saturday at 9:00 a.m. sharp.

Leonard I won't be here next week because we are leaving Sunday for my grandmother's. She's not doing well so I appreciate your prayers.

Harold Wow, I know it's a tough time for your family. We'll be praying for you. Let's all keep praying for the teens, the summer camp plans, the outreach next week, the GROWgroup Bible study…it's going well but we really want these teens to mature in faith…more prayer requests?

(The group circles up for prayer in closing. Harold and June leave immediately to get to Aleah's game but most of the others hang around for awhile. Leonard, Mary, and Izzy help clean up and load the dishes and then decide to go out to get something more to eat. After everyone leaves, Karen sits down with her husband, Ben to eat some popcorn and watch a movie. It is a team of diversity and unity; each used by God for His purposes to complete the task of reaching Deaf teenagers with the love and gospel of Jesus Christ.)

Those who are familiar with the DTQuest ministry recognize our high value on relationships. This is the strength of this team. They do not waste time on silliness. They work together with a common mission in mind—reaching Deaf teenagers with the love of God and gospel of Jesus Christ. The leadership time is not solely about planning but effective planning is important to a successful and sustainable ministry. Much of the planning should occur before the meeting. The Area Coordinator, or even a planning subcommittee, may accomplish this and put the finishing touches on the program with the full group. The point is that each member brings specific strengths to the mix. Some members are gifted at planning excellent programs. It is best to consistently have the same leader (who has gifts in proclamation) give the Biblical message. The point is that everyone contributes. Each role is important. The Scriptural message should always be the guiding theme for the entire event. At the core of the program is a group of leaders who care for each other and make sure each teenager is attended to and feels special and loved.

This fictional DTQuest leadership team reflects excellent diversity and unity. What if a leadership team is not diverse? Identify the deficits on the team and actively seek others to build a diverse team, but never at the expense of unity. There will always be seasons of balance and imbalance but this awareness helps maintain the importance of diversity. Pray for the Lord of the Harvest to bring diverse workers into the field. Always watch for potential new leaders especially those who round out your team and bring missing perspectives.

We must love as Christ has loved us. We must be willing to build bridges and not walls. God will bless our ministry, if we are willing to follow His commandments. We must love the Lord our God with all our heart, soul, mind and strength; and we must love our neighbors as ourselves. We must then take this faith and put it into action. The focus of the team is on the mission and not those things that divide us. We are the Body of Christ. As the Body of Christ, we become salt and light in the world. We let this light shine through our love for each other in Christ's name. It is God's Holy Spirit that adds *"to their number daily those who were being saved."* (Acts 2:47, NIV)

Jesus set his face towards Jerusalem

> *"Not long before it was time for Jesus to be taken up to heaven, he made up his mind to go to Jerusalem. He sent some messengers on ahead to a Samaritan village to get things ready for him. But he was on his way to Jerusalem, so the people there refused to welcome him. When the disciples James and John saw what was happening, they asked, "Lord, do you want us to call down fire from heaven to destroy these people?" But Jesus turned and corrected them for what they had said, 'Don't you know what spirit you belong to? The Son of Man did not come to destroy people's lives, but to save them.' Then they all went on to another village."* (Luke 9:51-56, CEV)[112]

This is a short and fascinating story in the Gospel of Luke about Jesus' journey to Jerusalem. The English Standard Version uses the phrase, *"He set his face to go to Jerusalem"* in verse 51. Jesus knew where He was going and why. There was a Samaritan village on the way that refused to welcome Him because the Jews and Samaritans generally hated each other. They resented that Jesus was going to Jerusalem. Brothers James and John (appropriately known as the *Sons of Thunder*) wanted to call down lightning on the village. They were not in a forgiving mood and wanted vengeance on these people.

Jesus *"made up his mind to go to Jerusalem"* (vs. 51) and because of his focus, the people in this Samarian town, *"refused to welcome him."* (vs. 53) They missed out on the blessings of having the Son of God as a houseguest. Jesus may have been saddened by their rejection but He stayed focused. He does not appear to be angry, in fact, Jesus expresses that His mission was to help people. He would not punish them. Neither would He fellowship with them. He simply went another way.

Jesus *"did not come to destroy people's lives, but to save them"* (vs. 55) and this is our quest. We come to Deaf teenagers as friends and messengers. We have experienced God's touch and want them to know of God's love. *All people* should have access to the Most, High God; all are welcomed to the One who saves. Language is no obstacle. Culture is no barrier. Jesus *"went on to another village"* (vs. 56) that was willing to accept Him. He stayed focused and on task.

Those involved in Deaf ministry during the Third Wave must figuratively set their faces *towards Jerusalem* and not be deterred by barriers, resistance, or rejection. The ministry should remain uncluttered. This ministry is not for hearing teenagers or for hearing people who want to learn sign language. This ministry is not solely for socialization. We want Deaf teenagers to have an opportunity to experience a personal relationship with God through Jesus Christ, grow in love of Scripture as authoritative and to develop a servant's heart through missions. We want them to become strong, independent Deaf men and woman who reflect the priorities of their Creator. These young people are the hope of the Deaf generation to come. They are the ones who will train their children *"in the way they should go"* (Proverbs 22:6, NASB) and to love God, neighbor, and self. God has *set his face* to reconnect with the Deaf-World. Our responsibility is to love as we have been loved, to simply be honest about what we have experienced.

For the survival of an identifiable Deaf-World, there must be a rediscovery of meaningful religious experience. What happens if we neglect sharing God's incredible story with our children and youth? How do they face the challenges and struggles of life without any sense of faith in something greater than themselves? How can we develop a sense of self without turning and facing the One who created us? Where do we learn the difference between what is right and wrong? From where does one's internal moral compass come from, if not from the ultimate Judge? How does one understand the importance of personal relationships without knowledge of the One who created the very breath in our bodies?

The Deaf should have total and direct access to the Scriptures. They have the right to read, study, pray, worship, serve, lead, argue, discuss, and meditate on the word of God to decide for *themselves* what they believe about God. This is only reasonable. How did we get in such a predicament? How did we move from the Christian faith being such a vital part of the Deaf experience during the first half of the past century to this current crisis? In summary, it is because the paradigm has shifted and we are stuck in the past. We must be willing to change. God is able to reach any people group in the world. It is our responsibility to open our minds and hearts to His leading in this task. He wants his Deaf and hard of hearing children to know that He created them and wants a personal relationship with them.

In review, the foundation for effective and sustainable Deaf ministry…

- recaptures the rich faith traditions of Deaf-World through team based relational ministry that responds to the spiritual needs of the next generation
- creates new opportunities for Deaf to gather, interact, and connect with each other for enculturation of Deaf culture to continue and flourish
- adapts to the inevitable acculturation of language and culture with the dominant hearing world due to the scattering of the Deaf community
- recognizes the authenticity of a New Culture of Deafness that is emerging in the 21st Century in the United States

God has begun a revival and invites you to get involved. We are his hands and feet. We hope to relate to the roughest of characters with the kindest of actions. As Jesus stood on the beach while the demon-possessed man came screaming and running towards him[113], we are to reach into the lives of scared, crazy, teenagers with the calmness of the Savior who is in our hearts. His love is greater than their pain. Being flexible does not mean being weak. The good news is that God wins. Our job is simply to be faithful. Jesus looks at each one of us and says, *follow me.* No more words are needed. The master has called your name. Now, it is time to follow. It is Deaf time. May God bless you on your journey of faith. The adventure is great and the stakes are high. Someday, may you stand before our Lord and see Him smile and sign, *Finish! Wonderful. Good job!* (Thumbs up) *Finish!**

*"Well done, good and faithful servant."
Matthew 25:23, NIV

About the Authors

Bob Ayres

In the early 1980s, Bob and Kathy went as volunteer Young Life leaders on a backpacking trip to Colorado. When they arrived at camp, they met a Deaf teen that was with another group. After spending a week in the wilderness and returning home, their encounter with this Deaf teenager inspired a desire for the group to learn sign language. Along with the regular follow-up Bible study, they asked a friend, Terri Connolly, to provide sign language instruction for the group. This laid a foundation so that when Bob and Kathy moved to Georgia, they were able to communicate and become close friends with a Deaf couple whom they met at church, Charles and Janie Penland. Through this deep friendship, Bob and Kathy developed a love and appreciation for the Deaf experience and culture. Bob and Kathy Ayres have five children who were all adopted as older children. Their youngest daughter, Ana, is Deaf and from Ecuador. She was adopted in 1993 when she was eight years old.

Bob's professional life has been focused primarily on establishing new ministries and human service organizations. He was the director and teacher with the Christian Education Center (now called CenterPoint) in Gainesville, Georgia. For five years, he was the Executive Director of the Brain Injury Association of Kentucky. He has a Master of Religious Education (1983) and a Master of Education (1992). Bob has written extensively, published many articles, and contributed to two books on youth ministry. He is the author of *Real-Life Wisdom: Stories for the Road* published in 2004 by iUniverse Press. The Ayres are both nationally certified sign language interpreters. Bob and Kathy founded DeafYouth Ministries in December 2000. Bob serves as President/CEO and member of the Board of Trustees. Kathy is actively involved in the local DTQuest ministry in Louisville, Kentucky where they reside.

Chad Entinger

Chad Entinger was born in Edina, Minnesota. Chad became deaf when he was sixteen months old when he contracted Spinal Meningitis. He was raised by

Christian parents in Howard Lake, Minnesota. Chad was mainstreamed through junior high. He then went to high school at the Minnesota State Academy for the Deaf, graduating in 1993. He graduated from Gallaudet University in Washington, D.C. with a Bachelor of Arts degree in Elementary Education in 1997 and a Master of Arts degree in Deaf Education in 1999.

Chad and Glory (formerly Somerville) were married in Fruita, Colorado, in 2001. They have two children, Shekynah Ann and Corban Peter. Chad has extensive experience working with Deaf, hard of hearing, and hearing youth at various schools, programs, camps, and conferences.

Chad has acted in several video productions including the *Finger Food Café* and *Daily Devotions for the Deaf: Sign Language Edition*. He also created Deaf Missions' *Hands for Jesus Kids' Club* and authored several printed materials related to family and youth. He is a teacher of the Deaf and coaches football at the Minnesota Academy for the Deaf in Faribault, Minnesota. Chad enjoys being with his family and Deaf teenagers. Public speaking, watching and playing sports (especially football!), reading, and writing are among his favorite hobbies.

Bibliography

Claggett Statement. Mennonite Board of Missions, Goshen, IN: [Video only in ASL], 1984. Read transcript only.

Erikson, Erik. *Identity: Youth and Crisis.* New York: Norton, 1968.

Gannon, Jack. *Deaf Heritage: A Narrative History of Deaf America.* Silver Springs, MD: National Association of the Deaf, 1981.

Gray, D., Lewis, G., and Lewis, G.A. *Yes, You Can, Heather! The Story of Heather Whitestone, Miss America, 1995.* Grand Rapids, MI: Zondervan, 1995.

Green, Chip. *Handbook for Deaf Ministry* (unpublished).

Lane, Harlan. *The Mask of Benevolence: Disabling the Deaf Community.* San Diego, CA: DawnSignPress, 1999.

Lane, Harlan. *When the Mind Hears: A History of the Deaf.* New York: Random House, 1989.

Lane, H., Hoffmeister, R., and Bahan, B. *A Journey into the DEAF-WORLD.* San Diego, CA: DawnSignPress, 1996.

Lawrence, Marshall (Ed.). *Shattering the Silence: Deaf and Hard-of-Hearing Christian Speak Out About the Church.* Elkhart, IN: Silent Blessings, 2001.

Meredith, Char. *It's A Sin to Bore a Kid: The Story of Young Life.* Waco, TX: Word Books, 1978.

Sampley, DeAnn. *A Guide to Deaf Ministry: Let's Sign Worthy of the Lord.* Grand Rapids, MI: Zondervan, 1990.

Spradley, Thomas, and Spradley, James. *Deaf Like Me.* Washington, DC: Gallaudet University Press, 1985.

Stassler, Barry (Ed.). DeafDigest. An online newsletter of information for the Deaf community.

Stewart, D., Schein, J., and Cartwright, B. *Sign Language Interpreting: Exploring its Art and Science.* Boston: Allyn & Bacon, 1998.

Whitestone, Heather and Hunt, Angela. *Listening With My Heart.* New York: Galilee Trade, 1998.

Endnotes

[1] The World Book Dictionary, 1992.

[2] Lane, Hoffmeister, Bahan. *A Journey into the Deaf-World.* DawnSignPress. 1996. This authors did not necessarily coin the phrase but put it into written form, Deaf-World.

[3] Conversion does not necessarily refer to conversion *from* atheism or another religion, rather, it is fundamental to the Christian belief that each individual must ultimately decide whether or not to receive Christ as Savior and follow Him as Lord.

[4] Jesus' conversation with Nicodemus recorded in the third chapter of the Gospel of John.

[5] This is an Old Testament concept of those who are true believers in God and will be delivered by His hand. The most clearly defined group were those in captivity in Babylon who were eventually returned to Jerusalem.

[6] There was a historic movement called Evangelicalism but I am referring to people of any denomination having a passion for others to come to know Christ.

[7] I have a particular fondness for this term but it is too general for our purposes here.

Deaf Diaspora: Scattered Community—Chapter 1

[8] The Interpreter's Dictionary of the Bible, "Dispersion." pp. 854-846

[9] This is a summary definition based on The World Book Dictionary, "Diaspora" with application to the Deaf community added in the form of an example.

[10] There is a theory that deafness is the result of a recessive gene but this thought is not commonly accepted in the scientific community.

[11] This is a difficult estimate to quantify but well established that very few hearing parents of Deaf children ever reach true fluency in American Sign Language.

[12] Exodus 24:6-8 is one example of this concept as a people with a direct agreement with God to be His people and He will be their God. This is why they are called the Chosen People.

[13] www.consumingfire.com/native.htm

[14] www.historicaldocuments.com/IndianRemovalAct.htm

[15] This is a reference to a book by Alex Bealer about the Trail of Tears; the forced removal of the Cherokee Nation in 1837 from Georgia and the Carolinas to reservations in the mid-west. On this cruel journey, one-in-four of the people died and it essentially signaled the end of their culture.

[16] U.S. Department of Commerce, Native American Economic Development, learn more at www.commerce.gov

17 www.consumingfire.com/native.htm

18 Department of the Interior, Bureau of Indian Affairs. Federal Registry. Vol. 67, N0. 134. July 12, 2002.

19 Department of the Interior found at www.ost.doi.gov/linksfaqs/links_faq.html

20 Census 2000 found at www.census.gov

21 There has been a recent revival occurring in the Native American world. The National Museum of the American Indian had their grand opening at their location on the mall in Washington, DC in September, 2004. Check out more information about the museum online at americanindian.si.edu

22 Learn more at the Kwanzaa Information Center at www.melanet.com/kwanzaa

23 I make the assumption that the reader is at least somewhat familiar with the cultural perspective of deafness and although we will explore this subject more in depth during the next chapter, I do not try and build a case for this belief. Deafness as a cultural experience is well-documented in the academic world.

24 Mitchell and Karchmer, "Chasing the Mythical Ten Percent: Parental Hearing Status of Deaf and Hard of Hearing Students in the United States." Accepted for publication in *Sign Language Studies* in 2002.

25 Stewart, Schein, Cartwright. *Sign Language Interpreting: Exploring its Art and Science.* 1998.

26 www.knesset.gov.il

27 The covenant that God made with Abraham in Genesis 15 (and in other places) promising to give him many descendents and a promised land for them to become a great nation.

28 Lane, Harlan. *When the Mind Hears: A History of the Deaf.* First Vintage Books. 1984. p. 6.

29 Ibid.

30 Ibid. These are the imagined words of Laurent Clerc in describing his experience at the National Institution for the Deaf in Paris.

31 Gannon, Jack R. *Deaf Heritage: A Narrative History of Deaf America.* National Association of the Deaf, 1981. p. 16.

32 Ibid, p. 181-183.

33 The Lutheran Church official website at www.lutheran.com

34 *Deaf Heritage*, p. 46-47.

35 Ibid, p. 47.

36 The Congress of Milan was a terrible assault on the Deaf way of life in its rigid promotion of strict oralism in the education of Deaf children. This connection to the sudden decrease in Deaf priests in the Anglican church is pure speculation on my part but certainly would make for interesting research.

37 This is a phrase coined by me. I think it reflects the radical nature of God's love for His people.

38 March of Dimes, Quick References and Facts Sheets, 2002.

39 Lane, Hoffmeister, Bahan. *A Journey to DEAF-WORLD*. DawnSignPress, 1996. p. 230-231.

40 Ibid, 128-130.

Deaf Diaspora: Deaf-World—Chapter 2

41 Lane, Harlan. *The Mask of Benevolence: Disabling the Deaf Community*. DawnSignPress, 1999. p.18-19.

42 Dr. Bahan is Deaf and the chairperson of ASL and Deaf Studies at Gallaudet University.

43 Dr. Hoffmeister is a CODA (Child of Deaf Adults) and was raised on the campus of the American School for the Deaf where his parents were teachers. He is an associate professor at Boston University in the department of Developmental Studies and Counseling and director Deaf studies.

44 Lane, Hoffmeister, Bahan. *A Journey to DEAF-WORLD*. DawnSignPress, 1996. p. 124.

45 Ibid

46 Ibid

47 Ibid

48 Ibid, p. 125

49 Ibid

50 Ibid

51 The commonly-held definitions of the meaning of Deaf culture are being challenged by this book (*Deaf Diaspora: The Third Wave of Deaf Ministry*) as we move into the new century. Sampley uses a definition of Deaf culture prevalent at that time.

52 Stassler, Barry. DeafDigest. December 21, 2003—February 1, 2004.

53 The term "Culture Shock" was introduced in 1958 to describe the anxiety experienced when first moving into a completely new environment.

54 The Purpose-Driven Church is a ministry of Saddleback Church in Lake Forest, CA and has been used by thousands of churches for discipleship and church growth. More information is available at www.purposedriven.com

55 Deaf Queer Youth. *Youth Resource* is a website developed for this purpose. Deaf Youth Rainbow was incorporated in 1997.

56 Carlson, Tara. LeGIT SIG Update. VIEWS (RID). Vol. 20, Issue 11, December 2003.

57 Barry Strassler. DEAFDIGEST email newsletter. October 19, 2003

Deaf Diaspora: Crisis REAL—Chapter 3

58 Barry Strassler. DEAFDIGEST email newsletter. December 7, 2003

59 A term coined by Dr. Tom Humphries in 1975 that is in use within the academic community but has not yet been incorporated into the dictionary. More information is available at www.audism.org

60 http://www.ssa.gov/notices/supplemental-security-income/

61 Lane, et al, p. 135

62 There are a number of books and articles on this subject. We used an article by Dennis L. Okholm, "I Don't Think We're in Kansas Anymore, Toto! Postmodernism In Our Everyday Lives." Theology Matters. Volume 5, Number 4, July/August 1999, www.theologymatters.com

Deaf Diaspora: Next Generation—Chapter 4

63 At the time of the writing of this book, DePaul University was developing "Paula," an animated interpreter on a monitor to be used initially in security settings such as airports. It would allow for verbal input that is interpreted into ASL.

64 quest4arts.org/productions/deafway2

65 www.deafway.org

66 www.marleeonline.com

67 Williams, John. "Assistive Technology." May 23, 2001. www.businessweek.com

68 www.heatherwhitestone.com

69 Berke, Jamie. What You Need to Know About (website). www.deafness.about.com

70 The slogan from the show *Survivor* seen on CBS.

71 www.amazingchristy.com

72 Ibid. This show is being produced by Versatile Productions in Carbondale, CO.

73 Chip Green tells of examples of this in his book, *Handbook for Deaf Ministry* to be published.

74 The term has become more formalized in terms of a movement but refers to a priority of putting faith into action in arena of justice issues such as hunger, poverty, and social inequity. One criticism of this approach to faith is the potential to become a "works" belief system that is focused on the salvation of societies more than individuals.

75 Mr. Roy Holcomb graduated from Gallaudet University in 1947. Later he earned four master's degrees in from the University of Tennessee, Ball State University, and the California State University—Northridge. He held positions as a teacher and administrator in a number of settings including the South Dakota School for the Deaf, the Santa Clara County Office of Education, the Sterch School in Delaware, and the California School for the Deaf in Fremont.

76 BEGINNINGS For Parents of Children Who Are Deaf or Hard of Hearing, Inc. www.deafness.about.com

77 Patterned Language was originally developed by Mr. B. J. Peck, past director of the Oregon School for the Deaf in Salem, Oregon.

78 www.gmdeaf.org/pl/pl_mission.html

Waves THREE: Second Wave—Chapter 6

79 www.ada.gov

80 http://pr.gallaudet.edu/dpn

81 Claggett Statement. Mennonite Board of Missions, Goshen, Indiana. [Video recording]. 20 min., ASL only, no voice.

82 From the Silent Blessings website at www.silentblessings.org

83 www.deafmissions.org

84 Colin Bruner, a pastor with the Deaf in Louisville, Kentucky was the source of this information

85 Mark's website address is http://markmitchumweb.home.att.net/index.htm

86 From the Deaf Ministries Worldwide website at www.deafminstries.com

87 Information about storying can be found at www.chronologicalbiblestorying.com

88 www.doorinternational.com

89 Youth Specialties can be found on the web at www.youthspecialties.org and the National Network of Youth Ministries is located at www.nnym.org

90 www.younglife.org and www.yfc.org

Waves THREE: Third Wave—Chapter 7

91 Steve Cocheo, Executive Editor of American Bankers Association's ABA Banking Journal on-line, March 1997.

92 *The American Heritage® Dictionary of the English Language, Fourth Edition Copyright © 2000 by Houghton Mifflin Company.*

93 John 13:1-17

94 Matthew 9:12, Mark 2:17, Luke 5:31, NIV

95 This is a concept that I developed. It is explained more in depth in Chapter 8.

96 Sandy Kilgo with Christian Deaf Fellowship and the Christian Deaf Virtual University was the source of this information. Learn more about this exciting option for training at www.d-e-a-f.com

97 John 10:10

98 Based on Erikson, Erik. *Identity: Youth and Crisis.* 1968.

[99] Of course, it is also important to be able to relate adequately with the opposite gender as part of a group but this should have occurred during an earlier stage. The key is learning to be "in love" with an individual without losing a healthy sense of self or impairing the other person's sense of self. Success in this task can be generalized to the opposite sex as a group and to future relationships.

[100] This concept was developed by Bob Ayres for DTQuest Orientation in 2002.

[101] This is the title of his book that describes the founding and philosophy of *Young Life*.

[102] By Gary Portnoy and Judy Hart Angelo

[103] www.yfc.org

[104] www.younglife.org

[105] www.nnym.org

[106] www.youthworker.com

Vision IMPACT: The DTQuest Model—Chapter 9

[107] Ayres, Robert. Summary of Field Education Objectives; Competency Statement #5 for a class at Southern Baptist Theological Seminary in Louisville, KY. September 14, 1982

[108] Those who are part of Deaf culture tend to have an interest in how a hearing person became involved in Deaf-World and what one's background is. I started with this section in respect of this time-honored tradition and to express my deep love and appreciation to the Penland family.

[109] This material comes from the DTQuest Area Coordinator Training Manual written by Bob Ayres

[110] Steve Dye was an Area Coordinator for DTQuest-Greater Louisville and through consultation with Bob Ayres and Rev. Tim Bender (a Deaf Southern Baptist minister), Steve led in the establishment of the Deaf Café ministry. Steve Dye is to be given full credit as the founder of the Deaf Café ministry. Deaf Café follows many of the same principles as DTQuest but has the ultimate goal of establishing local Deaf churches focused on young adults. The larger vision is for Deaf Café to spread across the country and regional workshops are in the plans. Deaf Café is a name coined by Bob Ayres and used to describe a coffee-shop atmosphere showcase event on Friday nights at the Deaf Teen Ministry National Symposium and also one of the activities at the DTQuest summer camps. The name has now been conferred to this specific ministry for their unlimited use. May God continue to bless this exciting new ministry!

Vision IMPACT: Conclusion—Chapter 10

[111] This is a Deaf song written by Lisa Frey and Stacy Wildes in 2003.

[112] Part of verse 55 was included from a footnote that was part of some of the early manuscripts. It explains the first part of the verse so I included it in the quotation.

[113] Luke 8:26-39

0-595-33541-1